It Could
Have Been Worse

It Could Have Been Worse

PEGGY HOLMES

Aided and abetted by JOY ROBERTS

COLLINS
TORONTO

First published 1980
by Collins Publishers
100 Lesmill Road, Don Mills, Ontario

Canadian Cataloguing in Publication Information

Holmes, Peggy, 1898—
  It could have been worse

ISBN 0-00-216612-7

1. Holmes, Peggy, 1898—   2. Pioneers — Alberta —
Biography.   I. White, Joy Roberts.   II. Title.

FC3673.1.H64A3   971.23′02′0924   C80-094226-4
F1078.H64A3

Printed in Canada

To Harry, my liberator,
who piloted me
through sixty years
of matrimony.

And to my son,
Bryan.

Passions and urges, long since stilled,
Ashamed to think we e'er indulged.
Heavens would fall should we declare
We enjoyed it all.

PEGGY HOLMES,
The Sexless Seventies

Contents

Illustrations between pages 80-81 and 112-113

Foreword

I have known Peggy Holmes for only three years, although I had been a regular listener to her CBC broadcasts telling of her pioneer days just after the First World War.

When I asked her why she didn't write a book, she confessed that she didn't know where to start or how to tackle nearly a hundred years of living life to the full. She told me she had trunks full of penciled scribblings made when she was homesteading in northern Alberta, so together we have sorted out her life story from her birth in 1898 until the day she returned to city life in 1923. Now aged 82, she is the oldest broadcaster in Canada, and is still airing her scripts on CBC.

She has so many stories to relate, some sad and some hilarious as she has always maintained her keen sense of humour. It is a great privilege to work with this gracious lady, who is loved by young and old alike.

To see Peggy typing out her scripts on her 65-year-old typewriter, and dashing around Edmonton in her Datsun stationwagon, makes one realize that senior citizens have a lot of living to do.

JOY ROBERTS

Acknowledgements

"Joy to my world has come." On the last day of 1976 Joy Roberts, with her experience, and creative juices flowing at full tide, offered to collaborate with me on publishing my memoirs. Without Joy my scribblings would have died in cartons.

All through the years wonderful friends and teachers have come into my life, each of whom has helped to create the mosaic which has now come into focus.

Among the many I would like to thank are: Elsie Park Gowan from whom I took my first creative writing lessons; Jackie Rollans who gave me my first broadcasting assignments; and Dorothy H. Gray who assisted with proofreading and research.

PEGGY HOLMES

1
Undaunted Optimism

As I tried to relax on the hard, springless wagon seat, jogging over the rough trail taking me to my new life in Canada, I glanced up at my husband.

Could this possibly be the man I'd married only four years ago in England? Even though I knew he owned property in northern Alberta, I had never had any burning desire to be a wild west pioneer, and when I repeated my altar vow, "For better, for worse", such a drastic change in my lifestyle was beyond my wildest dream.

Mile after mile we bumped along through the deep ruts and mud holes, past the odd slough and over muskeg. The corduroy track of felled poplar trees was bordered by a row of dark green spruce standing like sentinels. It was scary!

As the wagon hit an extra large bump I was knocked off the seat and out of my reverie.

"How many more miles to your homestead, Harry?" I enquired. "Only twenty more", he replied comfortingly.

We were now ten miles from the end of steel at Ashmont where we had stopped overnight.

I received my first shock when a kindly soul took me aside and asked, "Do yer know what you're doing going alone into the bush like that? Yer 'usband looks more like one of them poets than a farmer."

Of course I knew what I was doing. Harry had survived four years of trench warfare in the army. Surely he could measure up to clearing some bushland with my help!

As we continued our bumpy journey along the track between piles of burning brush, where

15

groups of homesteaders were clearing their land, the acrid smoky smell and crackle of the flames took me back to my childhood and a fire which had changed my whole life.

As I think back, my life has been a jigsaw puzzle, many pieces, big and small, which are all coming together now I am eighty-two. It's rather ironic that I am only now, in my new career as a writer, reaping the benefits from the tough years on our homestead which, happy and eventful as they were, left us practically penniless.

But fate has always played a big part in my life. There have been so many strange incidents — even the change of my name — and looking back, I can't think how anything could have been different.

My first encounter with fate was a fiery inferno which destroyed our home in Hull, England, in 1913. After that, my conventional childhood was never the same.

That was the night my mother and I decided to go to the "flicks". We threw on our old tweed coats, as in those days our best clothes were kept sacred for Sundays.

We had a most enjoyable time, weeping copiously with Norma Talmadge in *Camille*. That wonderful actress could really turn on our waterworks. During those days of silent movies the background music was supplied by a piano player in the pit, who invariably rendered *Hearts and Flowers* during the tear-jerking scenes, which further whipped up our emotions.

As we turned the corner leading to Beverley Road where we lived, we saw a huge orange cloud lighting up the sky. For a few seconds it didn't dawn on us that it was our own home going up in flames.

The bright red fire engines, drawn by horses,

clattered past us. The firemen in their big black helmets, ankle-length coats, and squelchy Wellington boots were busy unrolling the fire hoses by hand. The water was carried in a tank on one of the trucks, as there were, of course, no fire hydrants in those days.

We rushed towards the scene in panic. Mother said she remembered leaving some washing in front of the fire to air. As our overmantel was artistically draped in velvet with a heavy ball fringe, it was a regular fire hazard and we figured that it had caught ablaze and had started the fire.

The shutters had been securely drawn over the windows, so the house had been closed in and the fire must have been smouldering for some time. It wasn't until my father returned from his club and opened the front door that the flames burst out on him, and the whole interior was by then an inferno.

I was very dramatic and wanted to race into the house immediately to save some of our possessions. I rushed past one fireman screaming, "I must go in. I live here."

But a large hand pushed me back. "Like 'ell yer do, miss, not in this bleedin' mess." Firemen were not very polite in those days!

Feeling slightly sick, I stepped back into the crowd. Many friends and neighbours had arrived by this time. They gathered around us, clucking with sympathy. I began to feel like Grace Darling or Joan of Arc.

The vicar's wife, a small bird-like woman, quickly appeared on the scene bearing a large jug of hot soup. She always had a stock on hand for the poor of the parish. Many of the men would probably have preferred beer, but the whole crowd seemed to enjoy the excitement.

Mother, of course, was broken hearted, as she

17

had lost all her sentimental and valuable treasures, one of her most prized possessions being a wedding present, a gigantic Wedgwood cheese dish and cover. I used to hate the odour of the ripe Stilton as the lid was lifted.

The worst disaster for me was the loss of my piano. My father had just bought me a new one, and I prayed that it would be spared as I fondly imagined myself being a famous concert pianist one day.

But the day after the fire, when I could get into the house, all that remained was what looked like a row of chocolate bars, and as I touched it, it crumbled. So there ended my pianoforte career, although I continued to take singing lessons, thinking I might be a prima donna instead.

As the house was brick, the solid walls still stood, but all the woodwork was charred, and the interior was a sorry sight.

I didn't realize at the time how much our possessions had meant to my mother. Apart from the piano, I was secretly rather pleased that the old stuff had gone. I had always hated dusting the whatnot. Thank heavens I wouldn't have to do that again!

Mother decided to stay with her parents who lived nearby until the house could be restored. I could have gone with mother and dad, but I had so many tempting invitations from school friends that I preferred to make my own choice. Being an only child I was often very lonely; I wanted to be where there was lots of excitement.

While I was trying to make up my mind where to live while our home was being rebuilt, Phyllis Holmes, my favourite friend, said, "Why don't you come to us, Peggy?"

This I thought was a marvellous idea, as Phyllis lived what I considered an ideal life. Her mother had run away with another man, her father was a recluse, and the house was run by an elderly housekeeper who was anything but strict, so we could stay out as late as we liked. I remained there very happily for nearly a year, and for the rest of my youth I spent most of my time with the Holmes family.

Phyllis had three brothers. Ted was an organ builder in Scotland. Noel, the youngest, lived at home and worked in an office. The middle brother, Harry, was a cowboy on a ranch in western Canada.

Phyllis's older sister Cathy had just left school and was engaged to be married. She was very dark like a gypsy. Her father always introduced her as "my daughter with the lovely eyes and wobbly ankles."

Phyllis, who was three years older than I, was very tall and graceful with a face like a Madonna. She had a sweet disposition and saw everything through rose-tinted glasses, always finding a redeemable feature in everyone.

She also had a keen sense of propriety. At the time of a great tragedy in her life when her first love committed suicide, I remember her exclaiming, despite her grief, "Fancy, Peggy, he took his life on the front room rug!"

Phyllis was a romantic. She often used to tease me, saying, "Wait till Harry sees you. I'm sure he'll fall for you."

Apparently the finger of fate was pointing the way for me even then, because I did eventually marry her brother.

Phyllis, who played such a large part in my destiny, also changed my name. I was christened Maud, which some people pronounced with a broad Yorkshire "u". I hated the name, especially when they called me Maudie.

One evening the two of us went to the theatre to see *Peg O'My Heart*. The heroine was lighthearted like me, so Phyllis took one look at me and declared, "You're not Maud; you're Peggy, and I'm never going to call you anything else."

I was delighted, and I know my personality changed from then on.

When I broke the news at home that I was now Peggy, there was a heated family row. No way were they going to call me Peggy. I was christened Maud, and "Maudie" I was going to remain. But I won out in the end and was known as Peggy by everyone except one stubborn aunt!

When I arrived on the North American continent I realized even more why I was glad I had changed my name. Every mule seemed to be called Maud!

2
Premonitions

I used to visit my grandparents often. They were very fine people and I loved them dearly.

Grandfather Waite, my mother's father, was a ship's chandler. He owned an ironmonger's shop in Hull, which we now call a hardware store. He had a big workshop at the rear with a separate glass house where the glaziers worked, making and repairing windows. There were several employees, including two apprentices, working under a foreman, John Fish, known to everyone as "Old John". It was a very busy and exciting place.

Old John was a great favourite with the kids. He

could make or mend anything, and would often clean out the huge workshop so we could hold a sale and tea for our various charities.

John Fish was so loyal to my grandparents that he refused to retire even when he was left a legacy. His favourite pastime was to display the medal he received from the British government for sixty years loyal service to the Waites.

Grandpa was a slight, dapper man with bright blue eyes, who moved very quickly and took off like a kite. He was a lovable character, always happy. Children followed him as if he were the Pied Piper of Hamelin, mostly because he always had a pocketful of pennies and candies. He came from a wealthy family and received a quarterly allowance.

Grandfather loved to go to fairs, and Hull was noted for its big annual fair to which people flocked from all over the country. His business was near the cattle market and he enjoyed the sales.

He also liked visiting the docks but he never went to sea. He was well known by the captains and seafaring men, but he refused to accompany them on any trips although he was often invited. He had a very good reason. He was a terrible traveller and was seasick even when crossing the River Humber on a calm day. Once at a launching they managed to get him aboard and kept him on the ship for the maiden voyage. The few hours the vessel was away from shore grandpa was violently sick.

The joke was that he was made a Freeman of the City of Norwich, an honour inherited from his father who received it in 1830. Among the privileges were freedom "from all kind of Tollage, Pontage, Passage, Murage, Pannage, Rivage, Vinage, Lastage, Stallage, Pickage, Wharfage, Fossage, Carriage, and from all other Customs, in all the Sea

21

Ports throughout England, and in all others within the Dominions of our Sovereign Lord the King."

The most tangible of these privileges was that he could tie up his boat in any dock in the British Empire. The last thing my grandfather ever thought of was owning a boat. However this august title, which was handed down from oldest son to oldest son, died with him. His only son was killed in World War I.

Grandfather was an inveterate practical joker, but a very shrewd businessman. He was also a strict teetotaler. One day he amazed his friends when he was seen entering a pub during an auction sale. But he knew what he was doing. He bid for the counter. Everyone thought he was crazy, but it was solid pewter!

Another of his profitable ventures — although a rather gruesome one — was after the crash of the dirigible, the R-38, over Hull in the summer of 1920. Grandfather prudently bought the scrap metal from the wreck, melted it down in his workshop, and a cousin turned it into replicas of the airship in his munitions factory.

That was a terrible day in Hull. It was August 23, 1920, soon after my husband and I had left for Canada, when the dirigible, the R-38, blew up and split in two over the River Humber.

Strangely enough, I had been having premonitions about something terrible happening in my home town, and as the war was over I couldn't imagine what it could be. I wrote to my parents immediately to see if they were all right — even before I had heard of the disaster. As they had been among the spectators they were able to give me graphic details.

After the success of the R-34 which had crossed the Atlantic both ways, the United States government ordered a similar dirigible to be built in Howden, Yorkshire, for the United States Navy. The R-38, a copy of the German zeppelin, was rechristened the ZR-2 and was painted with the American colours. It had passed all its tests and was on its last trial flight with a combined United States Navy and Royal Air Force crew when the disaster occurred.

The airship had been flying for many hours in heavy fog, but by late afternoon the sun broke through and it glided over Hull. It was a peaceful sight after the many zeppelin raids the city had suffered during World War I.

But around five thirty p.m. the nose of the ship fell, and some of the spectators thought she was coming down to give them a better look.

Then there was a terrifying explosion which shook the entire city, and it looked as if the airship was going to drop into the middle of the crowded business section. People ran madly for cover and several were knocked to the street by the concussion. However, the ZR-2 dived towards the river, and Hull was saved from a major catastrophe.

A second explosion followed, and a large split appeared in the centre. The crew started jumping, some with their parachutes open. The forward part caught fire at the break and the airship broke completely in two, both portions plunging into the river five hundred yards from the pier.

It hit a spit in the river, known as the little sandbank, where Phyllis and I had been stranded overnight in a yacht with two young men a few years previously, an episode which had caused my family much dismay as they feared we had suffered a fate worse than death!

Tugs and small boats hurried to the wreck. Rescuers tried to reach the crew with boat hooks, but the bodies were swept away by the tide and were hidden by a wall of flames.

Only a handful of survivors remained. Most had

been trapped inside the airship. One of the lucky ones was Lieutenant Richard E. Byrd who had been appointed navigator for the trans-Atlantic trip. He had missed his train in London and was hurrying to the base by taxi just as the airship took off from Howden. It was his sad task to identify the bodies and attend to the funeral arrangements. This man later became the famous polar explorer, Admiral Byrd.

I have always had what some people call "second sight", and many strange things have happened to me. One manifestation — if you can call it that — took place recently at a banquet in Ottawa when I was sitting next to Walter Turnbull, former personal secretary and adviser to the late Prime Minister Mackenzie King.

We were discussing Mr. Mackenzie King's séances and his contacts with the other world, although Mr. Turnbull told me he did not take part in any of them. I was beginning to feel slightly "disembodied" when a strange thing happened. We heard a thud on the floor, and Mr. Turnbull, thinking I had dropped my purse, dived under the table to retrieve it.

Then I saw a flower lying in my lap. It was a red and white carnation tied with a bow. No one around us was wearing a corsage, and the table decorations did not contain carnations. Seeing the funny side as usual, I remarked complacently "a gift from Mackenzie King."

But the mystery remains to this day and I still have the withered flower among my possessions.

All my life I have had strange premonitions. When I was very young I was told that an old aunt of mine was a "seer" and was "very queer". I didn't think she was queer at all, but I had to keep a lot of my feelings to myself. It was only later in life that I knew I was psychic.

3
Early Women's Lib

Both my grandparents were staunch supporters of the Church of England, and St. Thomas's Church in Hull was built mainly owing to their support.

Grandmother Waite was taller than grandfather. She sailed along like a battleship, and was a most determined woman. She was not intimidated like so many women of the time, and often after dinner at our home when my grandfather would say, "Come along Nellie, it's time to go," she would remain firmly seated. She went only when she was ready, sometimes two tramcars or wagonettes later.

But although outwardly severe, she could see through people, and she had a great empathy for anyone in trouble. She was a patron of the Blind Institute in Hull, and nearly every week one of us had to go to the Institute to bring home a blind girl for the weekend.

Emmie, one of our blind friends, was a wonderful person. My grandmother first saw her weaving baskets in the window of the Blind Institute. Both she and grandfather helped Emmie financially and later sent her to London where she became a successful masseuse.

Grandmother was not only determined but an individualist, especially in her choice of clothes. In those days women wore bonnets with ribbons tied under their chins. But she was definitely avant-garde with her turned-up hat trimmed with broad ribbons and a big jaunty bow at the side.

However one day even that became too much for her. Taking out the scissors, she chopped off her bow, remarking "This is just a lot of nonsense!"

I was good at "diddling-up" hats as I worked at a milliners for awhile. So when grandmother called me one day and announced, "Now, my child, I am going to a funeral and I need a new hat," I fixed up what I considered a most suitable creation in black. But she descended on me crying, "This is altogether too melancholy! Get rid of those ribbons and give me some flowers instead!"

It was then I knew grandma would carry out her own ideas whatever other people might think. Some of her friends even copied her, which seemed to release them from their traditional inhibitions. They began to loosen-up and assert themselves, at last realizing that they were humans, not chattels.

Every Sunday my grandparents attended church, returning at noon for lunch with members of the family including my young cousins. After an interminably long grace, we children were always given the same advice, "Those who eat the most pudding will get the most meat." So we tackled the suet pudding first, thus stretching the meat course to miraculous proportions. What a good idea for people with large families; a good helping of "spotted dog" or Yorkshire pudding and gravy first, and you are then too overwhelmed to tackle the meat!

Whatever the menu, grandfather would always say after every repast, "That's the best meal I've ever tasted, Nellie."

Grandmother prided herself on her Norfolk dumplings. Although she spent her married life in Yorkshire, she was born in the little village of King's Lynn, in Norfolk. In England nearly every county has its own special recipe. I remember grandma's dumplings as globs of uncooked bread dough dropped into an Irish stew or a soup, rolling around and looking anemic and unappetizing. But we had to eat them, and were constantly told about the starving Armenians and other underprivileged nations of the world.

Grandmother was also an expert with artichokes, and made her own caviar from fish roe. Her orange wine was another triumph, and she kept a few bottles until her youngest daughter was twenty-one. The family said it was better than champagne!

Both my grandparents had the digestions of mountain goats, and could eat anything at any time of the day or night. They were totally unaware of diets, and lived to be well over eighty years of age. If grandfather had a pain, grandma would dismiss it as the "collywobbles", saying reprovingly, "You had too many cockles and mussels before you came to bed."

Grandma was firm about human frailties. If she had the sniffles or a cold coming on, she would go down to the pier and take a trip on the ferry "to blow away the cobwebs". She had no use for folks who babied themselves. People were really stoic in those days. I remember being told about my great aunt Sally who had her breast removed. The doctor performed the operation on her dining room table. Aunt Sally was in her forties at the time, and lived until she was nearly ninety.

Grandmother also got on the wagon with the suffragettes, and even went to London to uphold the cause. I don't remember that she ever took an active part in a demonstration, but she certainly supported them in every way possible. One of the suffragettes under her banner was Emily Davison, who was killed at the Derby at Epsom in 1913 when she threw herself under a racehorse on the track.

Another link in my life chain was to find out several years later that Emily's husband had been a sergeant in Harry's regiment, the 31st Canadian Battalion. Harry was always generous with his

27

money, and he helped many of his army friends with loans. Sergeant Davison was one of the men who had borrowed ten pounds, but after the war their paths separated, and the two men lost touch.

Many years later, at a very low ebb in our finances on the Canadian homestead, I had the bright idea of making a list of all those who owed Harry money. The only man we could trace through the army records was Sergeant Davison, so we wrote and asked if he could see his way clear to repay the loan as we were broke. After several weeks, a reply came from his widow — he had married again. She informed us that her husband was dead and she was in dire poverty, but she would do her utmost to raise the money. Harry and I felt so sorry for her that we wrote immediately, cancelling the debt and enclosing a couple of dollars. We had only seven dollars to our name at the time! However, we decided to forget the possibilities of repayment from anyone, and to find some other way of getting hold of quick and much needed cash.

My grandfather's ancestors had come from the United States. His grandfather, Judge Newman Waite, had fought in the American War of Independence. The judge had a deaf mute daughter, but as there was nowhere in the United States at that time where this poor child could be educated, he brought his whole family to England and settled at Brammerton Hall in Norfolk. Mother, when she was a girl, remembered this old lady, her great-aunt, who talked in sign language, sitting by the fireside. She lived to be eighty-seven, and ended her days in my grandparents' home.

Over the years I can remember the times when unknown cousins arrived from the United States in search of some deeds. Apparently my great-great-grandfather had been granted some land on Broadway as a reward for his war services. But he had lost the deeds during his travels, and no one could ever locate them.

American relatives used to ransack my grandfather's house, taking the backings off the pictures on the walls to see if anything was concealed behind. But despite numerous searches nothing was ever found. The seekers were disappointed in their hopes of great wealth, as no doubt were my grandparents as they had always hoped they might get something out of this. Whether the land was Broadway in New York City or a place called Broadway we never knew. But it must have been a hot piece of property as the searchers made so many expensive trips from the United States to investigate.

I have very fond memories of my maternal grandparents, the Waites. I remember when grandfather said goodbye to me as I was leaving for Canada, he gave me a gold piece. In those days the men always carried golden sovereigns in their vest pockets.

Handing me the money, he said sadly, "My dear, I shall never see you again."

"Oh, don't talk like that," I replied. I didn't realize then that I was going so far away for so long. After all, I was only twenty-one.

But he insisted: "No, this is the last time I'll see you. It's wonderful that you are going to a new world, and so many strange things are going to happen to you. I wish I could live long enough to hear all about your exciting future."

Grandfather was indeed a prophet. I didn't believe him at the time, but his forecast was perfectly true.

4
Rhyme and Reason

Although much of my early life revolved around my grandparents, being an only child I was very close to my own parents. In fact I wasn't separated from them for very long as they both joined my husband and me in Canada after dad retired.

I never knew my grandfather Lewis as he died before my father was born. Dad was brought up by his strict older sisters who wanted him to be a little gentleman. They sent him to London and apprenticed him to a big interior decorating firm, then known as soft furnishings.

The poor little apprentices had to live in, and my father told me heart-rending tales about the appalling conditions. The food was meagre and tasteless. The boys had to be on the floor by seven thirty a.m. and the store remained open until nine p.m. every night except Saturdays when it closed at ten. No half days. My father said they really had to fight for half-day closing which was finally achieved by the formation of unions.

How on earth the young boys had enough spirit to joke I don't know. But they managed to get in a bit of fun during their dreary routine. One of their accomplishments was to master the art of pin flicking. Most of them worked on a balcony overlooking the main floor of the store, and competitions were held to see how many pins could be flicked into the head of a floor walker below, so that they stuck in his bald pate!

Dad worked in soft furnishings for a short while after his apprenticeship was completed. He frequently visited the stately homes of England to measure up for carpets and drapes, and advise on interior decoration. But it wasn't what he wanted in life, so he joined the post office and became manager of a Hull substation. When World War I broke out, he joined King and Company, suppliers of war equipment.

He always appreciated beautiful things, and when he was in soft furnishings he used to talk to me about various materials, and bring me samples of damask to feel. He gave me a good idea of colour and texture, which helped me later in life when I took up painting. It was, of course, part of my education.

My father also introduced me to sports, and took me to a football game every Saturday afternoon. He was an ardent supporter of the Hull City soccer team, the black and gold Tigers, and I've had a passion for soccer ever since.

He was also good at cricket, and continued to play even after he managed to get a ball in his mouth that took out his front teeth.

Grandfather was a rugby supporter, the Hull team being one of the roughest in the north. On Sunday after church both men had fiery arguments about the games.

Fortunately they were on the same side politically. We all wore a primrose and became members of the Conservative Primrose League. Dad also belonged to the Salisbury Conservative Club and was reputed to be one of the best billiard players in the country. We, of course, never saw him play, as women were taboo in his club.

It pays to have a funny father as I inherited his sense of humour which has helped me through many a tough spot. Dad won several national limerick competitions, one of his prizewinning efforts being:

There was a young lady of Bow
Who went for a walk in the snow.
When taking a stride
She trod on a slide
Unhinged was her "gait" don't yer know.

On another occasion he won first prize in a *John Bull* contest for the completion of a couplet. The editor at that time was Horatio Bottomley. The key line was "Lord Kitchener", to which dad added "England's Hidden Treasure". How true this turned out to be!

I wasn't very good at school as I couldn't see the writing on the blackboard. No one discovered I was shortsighted until I was about ten. So I had to have glasses which in those days, if you weren't good looking anyway, was the end! That was long before Dorothy Parker's "Men never make passes at girls who wear glasses."

I remember the optician saying to me when he placed the glasses on my nose, "Now, you must never, never take them off. If you do, you will have bad headaches. You'll have to wear them all your life."

I must have been a strong-minded little minx because I thought to myself, I don't believe you and I'm not going to.

When I came out of the optician's door I fell over the step as it seemed much nearer than it ever had before. So I took off my glasses and put them on just before I got home.

When I arrived at the house my father took one look at me. He exclaimed, "My poor child — good heavens!" Then he started to cry so I knew I looked an awful mess.

After that I wore glasses only when I had to look at the blackboard. I carried them in my pocket and frequently broke them. It was a costly affair. But I never had a headache and my eyes steadily improved so that when I was seventy-eight years old I passed the renewal test for my driver's licence with flying colours, and without glasses.

5
The Royal Sniff

When I was twelve I had an unpleasant experience. I hadn't been well for a few days and stayed away from school. So the doctor was summoned to check me over. Wearing his high silk hat and tail coat, and carrying his ebony cane, he arrived in his brougham with his coachman. His black bag was borne in ceremoniously. It was like having a visit from royalty.

Old Dr. Dowsing never gave anesthetics, just a silver sixpence if you didn't yell. It cost him a shilling to shut me up!

When he examined me he noticed that my toes were peeling slightly. Well, according to him, this was a sure sign of scarlet fever, and I was rushed to the isolation hospital where I remained for over a month.

Every day I was placed with several other kids on the side of a big bathtub where we had to sit dangling our feet in hot water. Their skin peeled off by the yard but none came off mine. I was fed to the teeth just sitting there trying to have the same symptoms as the others.

Eventually they allowed me to go home. The momentous day was my birthday, November 11, 1910. That morning when Dr. Dowsing came to sign my release my throat was very, very sore. I knew I was quite ill but no way was I going to let him know. I was just fine, I said. I was determined to get out of that place.

I always had a party on my birthday and when I arrived home I found that mother had arranged an extra big surprise for me to which all my friends had been invited. Somehow I staggered through it, but I was feeling really ill. By the time the last child had left I was delirious!

So I was rushed back to the fever hospital on a waterbed. Who says waterbeds are a new invention? This time it was definitely scarlet fever which it appeared I had never had in the first place but which I contracted in the hospital.

There was a big furore about it. Father was quite influential in the city and he declared he would expose the medical authorities. But they persuaded him that as I had scarlet fever and had to get better, he should say nothing about it. So he was allowed special privileges and was able to visit me, clad in a mask and white coat.

But it was a long haul, and when I recovered my parents said I had to go away for a holiday.

They decided to send me to Brighton to stay with my widowed aunt Alice, one of the sisters who had brought up my father. Her late husband, uncle Albert, had been a businessman in Leeds where he made medicine bottles. When he retired, the couple chose Brighton as it had the most suitable climate.

In 1910, a journey to Brighton from the north of England made one feel like a world traveller. People usually stayed put or holidayed nearer home. But I always loved adventure, and was tremendously excited when, with my ticket tied around my neck, I was put on the train in the care of the guard. I was met in London and put into another train for Brighton where my aunt was anxiously waiting for me at the station.

Although she had a twinkle in her eye, a mischievous trait that ran in the family, aunt Alice was a very strict Victorian lady and I had to behave myself. It was hard for me as I had had more liberty than most children of my age. But I used to sneak off when she was having a nap, and dash down to the beach to watch the people and the pierrots on the pier.

There were always exciting activities on the two piers, the Palace Pier and the West Pier, with Punch and Judy shows, orchestras playing, and other attractions including the "peep-shows" around which there was usually a cluster of gentlemen.

The bathing huts lined up along the beach were pulled to the sea edge by horses, and the ladies in their unrevealing suits modestly descended the steps into the water. Mixed bathing was not allowed, and the segregation of the sexes was clearly marked by large notices "Ladies' Bathing" and "Gentlemen's Bathing". I don't know if the two sexes ever met in the sea, but as the ladies were so timid I doubt if they ventured far.

I loved Brighton and all the ornate Regency buildings, especially the Royal Pavilion — an Arabian Nights' fantasy — with its big dome surrounded by smaller ones, which inspired a wag to remark, "St. Paul's has come to Brighton and pupped."

Aunt Alice was what you might call a snob. She was passionately devoted to anything or anyone connected with royalty. She followed the Court Circular avidly and knew just what every member of the Royal Family was up to — at least nearly all! I don't think she could keep up with King Edward VII. But all the old ladies in England, especially the spinsters, adored him and glossed over any hint of scandal connected with his august personage.

The highlight of my aunt's social activities occurred one day as she walked on the Marine Parade in Brighton with her little terrier, Lady.

As luck would have it, King Edward, who was staying with Sir Arthur Sassoon at Kings Gardens in Hove, was sitting in a shelter facing the sea with his constant companion, a terrier named Caesar.

My aunt was, of course, aware of protocol, but Lady had no such inhibitions and delightedly ran up to Caesar. The two dogs sniffed each other, played around, and became quite familiar! Aunt Alice blushed, but King Edward smiled, rose to his feet and raised his hat to her. He obviously approved of people — and animals — enjoying themselves!

When aunt Alice resumed her walk with Lady at her side, her head was held high. That royal sniff meant much to her as she had at last had a brush with royalty.

My aunt used to take me on long walks. One of our favourite routes was to Sussex Square where the Duchess of Fife lived on the corner. This was one of the fashionable squares where houseowners had the key to a private garden in the centre, from which a tunnel ran through to the private beach.

I used to peep through the railings and watch the Duchess's children and their friends playing. They were always accompanied by their nannies in starched dresses and caps. I thought how I would love to join them, just to jolly up the games which seemed rather tame.

6
The Milliner's Apprentice

I wasn't overly fond of school, and looked forward to the day when I could be released from bondage. During my last days there I took a domestic science course, which today is known as home economics. For this we had to cross the city to another school.

My great friend Ivy was an undertaker's daughter, and if there was no funeral on the day we went to science her father would send one of his open landaus, driven by a coachman wearing a tall black hat with a mourning ribbon hanging down the back. He and Horace, the horse, were a pair of gloomy souls.

Four of us took the trip in this landau and we were the envy of all the girls in the class.

Ivy held a big birthday party every year, and after tucking into a big meal we were sent to the coffin room to play. I didn't realize how macabre it was at that time, playing hide-and-seek in the coffins.

After these parties dad invariably recited to me an Irish ditty, the last word of which — even after sixty-seven years — I remember going like this:

> *His sister Mary Moffin*
> *Came and sat him in his coffin.*
> *His eyelids which were whoppers*
> *Did she decorate with coppers.*
> *He really looked quite fetching*
> *With the wadding on his chest*
> *And fit to mingle in the mansions*
> *Of the angels of the blessed.*

Eventually I persuaded my parents to allow me to leave school before graduating, as I wanted to join Phyllis at Marshall's, a fashionable milliners establishment on Brooke Street where she was learning the trade.

We apprentices paid no fee to learn, and received sixpence a week each for our labours.

The building was rickety and badly ventilated, with a big workroom at the top of a flight of creaky stairs. The girls sat around a long table with benches on each side. The one small window overlooked Moses the undertakers. The alley between the two buildings was so narrow we could almost shake hands with the boys making the coffins. We had to keep the window open because of the lack of air, so we had a lot of fun exchanging jokes back and forth.

As I was the last apprentice to be hired I wasn't given much to do. The girls brought me lurid novels to read aloud to them while they worked. When we heard our boss coming up the stairs I would throw my book into the big box under the table where we tossed in ribbon ends and scraps of material, grab a hat frame quickly and make believe I was working.

We were never allowed a telephone call unless there was a death or dire disaster in the family. I hadn't been there more than a couple of weeks when the phone rang for me. This caused a great commotion.

Mr. Marshall, with his mouth full of pins, ascended the creaking stairs calling, "Miss Lewis, you're wanted on the telephone." He escorted me downstairs and stood over me, breathing down my neck as he tried to listen to my conversation.

It was grandfather. He was always pulling my leg, and this time he merely phoned to ask, "How are you getting home tonight, dear?"

"I'm going on the tram," I replied.

"No, you mustn't", he said. "It's too dangerous. I will call for you."

"Why?" I whispered, Mr. Marshall's nose nearly touching my ear by this time.

"Well, you'll have your wages with you."

The wages were sixpence! But that was his joke.

When I hung up the phone Mr. Marshall asked what the trouble was.

I replied, "It was my grandfather. He wanted to speak to me but it wasn't important."

With a snort he departed. Such a thing had never before happened in his establishment.

I was considered a disturbing influence in the workroom so I was "elevated" to the salon downstairs where the results of our handiwork were on display. Here, the ladies came in their carriages to buy their millinery. This was quite entertaining, but when there was no one around I was bored, so I used to try on the old ladies' bonnets and the young girls' hats, dancing around the salon pretending I was on the stage.

Well, they caught me at that and I was fired. I wasn't too happy there anyway. I preferred reading love stories to the girls upstairs.

7
Big Business

Then came that shocking day, August 4, 1914, the outbreak of World War I. I was wondering what I could do in the way of war work when one day on the street I met an old friend of the family, Mr. Sholto Brown.

"You must come down to the bank where I

work," he said. "We're going to have to employ females when the men are called up. I'll give you an introduction."

"But I'm no good at figures," I protested. "I failed math in school."

"Oh, that doesn't matter," he replied. "You'll soon learn."

So I marched into the Union of London & Smith bank in Whitefriar's Gate and became the first woman bank employee in Hull. I don't think there were many others, if any, in England at that time.

By the time I left the milliners my wages had gone up from sixpence a week to two shillings and sixpence, but my first pay at the bank was a guinea — one pound, one shilling. I nearly went crazy. I really thought I was in the money!

Other girls were taken on as the men left, including Mr. Brown, and soon we had more women on the staff than men, just a few who were too old to enlist.

Most of the young male staff were training with Kitchener's army on the east coast a few miles away. They were amazed when we girls told them the jobs we were doing, posting ledgers, balancing cash, foreign exchange. They said they would be old men before they would ever have been able to rise to those positions.

Mathematics was my worst subject in school, and when I was nervous I couldn't add at all. I thanked God for my ten fingers and thumbs on which I used to count underneath the desk. We had no adding machines and only one typewriter. Everything had to be done in our heads. But I was surprised what I could do when I really had to.

It wasn't long before I was given a variety of tasks in the bank, one of them being a troubleshooter — looking for trouble, not being frivolous — checking to see that the figures balanced at the end of the day. If there was a discrepancy I had to report it, and we would have to balance to the penny before we left. It didn't matter if it took till midnight. If you were a penny out you had to find it, because that one penny might turn into a hundred pounds. Once we stayed all night before we discovered that one idiotic girl had added in the date at the top of the ledger.

The bank was large and dark as a morgue, a very depressing place in which to spend a lifetime. The manager was closeted in his private sanctum; one would not dare call it an office. We hardly ever saw him. He just limped out every once in a while to take a look around.

The assistant manager, Mr. Metcalfe, sat on a high rostrum in the centre of the room looking down upon us all. Nothing ever escaped him.

He was a crotchety old bachelor with thin hair scraped over a nearly bald pate, and a high stiff white collar. It was a terrifying experience to know that his hawk eyes were watching your every move. He hated women in the bank.

We sat on very high stools with no backs, and worked at slanting desks, entering figures in gigantic heavy ledgers which would give you a hernia to lift. Fortunately we were young and strong, and were able to help some of the frail old men who had spent most of their lives working in these surroundings. Looking back, I realize it was like something from Dickens.

We could never joke or talk. One day Mr. Metcalfe descended from his rostrum and called me to him. Piercing me with his beady eyes he snapped, "Miss Lewis, I cannot have blasphemous language in this establishment."

I was astonished until I learned that the reprimand stemmed from a report I had made in our time book. The Hull street cars were numbered on the front with letters, A for Anlaby, B for Beverley, and so on. I was late one day and had to write down why. I just put in the book, "The B car was late."

I suppose this period was the beginning of Women's Lib although we didn't know it. Former male employees, now in uniform, would drop in to see how things were going, and the bank became a sort of matrimonial bureau, not just a financial clearing house. Mr. Metcalfe, sitting up on high, frowned on those romances.

The zeppelin raids began while I was working in the bank. They looked like silver cigars suspended in the sky, and it was difficult to imagine that they were messengers of death.

Just before the first of the dreaded bomb attacks on Hull, we were informed that the city was very well fortified; we had no need to worry. We were also told that there were guns at the mouth of the River Humber, but the authorities lulled us to a sense of false security by omitting to tell us that they were wooden guns! Printed notices were circulated of the route we had to travel in case of invasion, as we had no air raid shelters. Our destination was the Cotswold Hills.

But the poor people who lived around Majors Tar Works merely fled into the parks and outskirts of Hull. It was a pitiful sight to see little families trudging along with their mattresses and a few cherished possessions on hand carts.

Hull suffered some damage, but it was nothing compared to the disaster some twenty-five years later when the city was gutted by high-powered enemy bombers in World War II.

I was still working in the bank when I first met my husband-to-be, and I remained there until after my marriage when I came to Canada with the first contingent of war brides in 1919.

8
The Wounded Hero

At last the time was drawing near for me to meet the famous Harry Holmes, whom I really felt I knew as Phyllis constantly regaled me with stories about her brother in Canada who was working on a ranch in the wild west.

"Why did he choose Canada of all places?" I asked incredulously, as I knew he had had an interesting job as personal assistant to Mr. Edgar Grotrian, editor of the *Hull Daily Mail*.

Phyllis told me that many long hours of working in a poorly lighted office had played havoc with his eyesight, and he was advised to give up close work for a while.

Roller skating was the craze at that time. Rinks sprang up all over Britain, the United States and Europe. Harry, who had learned to roller skate on a small rink in Hull, was appointed manager of the rink at Howden, Lincolnshire. Being an excellent skater and very popular, he was offered a position at the swanky American Roller Skating Club at Olympia in London, and later in Paris. Apart from a high standard of proficiency, the instructors had to be at least six feet tall, and he qualified in both respects.

Harry found this a very exciting life. On Sunday afternoons an exclusive actresses' club took over the rink. Each actress could choose her own instructor. Harry had the fascinating Dare sisters — Phyllis and Zena — who were the picture postcard beauties of the day.

But his favourite pupil was Fay Compton, a lovely red-headed girl, daughter of the famous actor Sir Edward Compton. She told him she was destined for the stage at an early age. She wrote to Harry for a time after she left England for boarding school on the continent. I guess she had a crush on him. He certainly had one on her!

Harry and I used to follow her stage and screen career and I remember, many years later, when we saw her on the TV screen as the old grandmother in the *Forsyte Saga* series, I realized with a shock the ravages of time on us all.

Harry gave up roller skating in 1911 and decided to emigrate to Canada. He spent a brief unhappy period in Ontario where he worked on a farm and, like many other green Englishmen, toiled for fifteen hours a day in the gruelling heat of summer for a mere pittance.

As soon as he had saved enough money he moved west to a ranch south of Calgary where life was more to his liking.

While there, he and three other ranch hands decided to go north on a moose hunt. They ordered stays and canvas from Eaton's catalogue, with which they converted a wagon box into a covered wagon, or prairie schooner as it was called.

They left Aldersyde in the fall of 1913 with a team of horses and enough guns and ammunition to start a small war, supplementing their food supplies with rabbits, partridge and prairie chicken.

It took them a week to reach Edmonton, and from there they followed the old Lac La Biche bull trail to St. Paul, then north to Vegreville which was then the end of steel. A further hundred miles and they were in moose country.

The appeal of this beautiful and vast no-man's land was irresistible, and finding it was available for homesteading, the four boys trekked back to the nearest land titles office and filed on a quarter section each. So Harry bagged a moose, a homestead, and later me!

While he was clearing the land around his new property and building a shack, he heard that war had broken out. He was so isolated that the news took a week to reach him. But he immediately shut the door of the little house he had just completed, and returned to Calgary to enlist in the 31st Canadian Battalion.

It was not long after Mr. Holmes had received the news that his son was a Canadian soldier, when he walked into the sitting room, with a stern face, holding a telegram.

"Phyllis my dear," he said. "Your brother Harry has been shot."

"Already?" we exclaimed. "Why, he hasn't left Canada yet."

We found out later that during arms instruction on the Calgary Stampede Grounds which had been turned into army headquarters, a soldier had been demonstrating with what was supposed to be an unloaded rifle. A bullet entered Harry's leg above the knee and hit the sciatic nerve.

So when the regiment was posted overseas, Harry Holmes embarked on crutches, making history by being the first casualty in the battalion!

9
Wartime Romance

My first meeting with Harry was in a romantic setting in the drawingroom of the Holmes' house. Here, in front of a blazing fire with his ancestors staring down at us from the walls, stood a tall, handsome soldier in Canadian uniform, which was much smarter than the British outfits.

We didn't fall in love at first sight as Phyllis had romantically predicted, but we were attracted to each other. I was ten years younger and admired his sophistication, while he was amused by my frivolous chatter and zest for life.

Harry's seven days leave passed all too quickly, with theatres, movies and family gatherings. Then it was back to camp for him and back to the bank for me.

A few months later he was granted another leave — but this was the dreaded overseas leave. It was then that we knew we were in love.

Harry wrote to me constantly from the trenches and I answered by return. Although he could not say much, we learned about the ghastly horrors of trench warfare from returned soldiers.

Phyllis and I searched the casualty lists daily, and sang the war songs, *Keep The Home Fires Burning*, and *The Long, Long Trail*. To keep up our spirits, we danced to *Alexander's Ragtime Band*, which was the rage at the time.

Meanwhile Harry was having a dreadful time in the mud of the trenches in France, amid the many fancy names given to the dugouts, such as Glory Hole, Lover's Lane, Suicide Corner, and the International Trench, which got its name because it changed hands so often.

In July 1915, when Harry was up to his eyes in mud, tunnelling under the German lines four miles from Messines Ridge, he was unexpectedly called to headquarters, where he was told he had been chosen to represent the 31st Battalion on Bastille Day, July 14. He was smartened up, given a new uniform, and sent to Paris for the ceremony where the troops were reviewed by King George V and Mr. R. B. Bennett, later Prime Minister of Canada.

But it was right back to the trenches after this welcome respite.

News from the war front became more and more alarming. Following the third battle of Ypres early in June 1916, came the death of Lord Kitchener who was drowned when the British destroyer HMS *Hampshire* was sunk when bound for Russia.

Then came the news we all dreaded to hear: Sergeant No. 79265 had been wounded. In mid-June Harry was made a company scout, spending every night in No Man's Land while his battalion held the front line. On August 10, 24 men of A Company were ordered to raid the German post and bring back a prisoner. Harry was appointed leader of the party, and all might have been well had not one of his men stumbled, allowing his bag of Mills bombs to roll off his back, which, of course, raised the alarm. Seven men were killed and seventeen wounded, and the mission was unsuccessful.

Harry heard the alert when he was up to the German parapet, and before he could retreat he was shot through the side of the head. Unconscious, he fell into a water hole, which actually saved his life as the shock of the cold water brought him round. He started to run, not knowing in which direction, when a bomb exploded just behind him, severely wounding him in the rear. He lay in the mud until the stretcher bearers were able to carry him out under cover of fire, and was brought back to England in a hospital ship, his face still blackened with the raid camouflage.

He underwent several operations, and the doctors dug out bolts, nuts, and bits of brass, which the nurses kept as souvenirs, but they were unable to get at three loose pieces of shrapnel which he carried all his life.

It was several weeks before he was released on sick leave, and returned to Hull in hospital "blues", the blue uniform which all the wounded wore. It was then that we became engaged to be married.

We went to Carmichaels, a fashionable jeweller in Hull, to choose a diamond ring with a beautiful rosebud setting. How I loved it — and still do! Every time I put it on, I think of that romantic day, March 10, 1916. Mr. Carmichael was a friend of the family and was very kind to us. Incidentally, he was the father of the famous British actor, Ian Carmichael, who, of course, was not born at that time.

When we decided to get married a year later, Harry's wedding leave was only forty-eight hours. So we were in a terrific whirl. We wanted the ceremony to be held on a Sunday in All Saint's Church just across the road from my home, which was destroyed in the Second World War when over half of Hull was flattened by enemy bombs.

The minister told us no weddings could be performed on a Sunday, but Harry quietly argued that it was a holy day and a holy ceremony, and he only had two days. He was so persuasive and logical that he won the day, and we tied the knot on Sunday, September 23, 1917.

It was a quiet family affair with a small reception at my home, as rations were limited. Also several close members of the family had suffered losses in the war in France which was still raging and looked as if it would never end.

Thousands of men were being killed daily, and the call came for every available soldier to be sent to the front. Harry, who was a sergeant-instructor on the Lewis gun, was recommended for a commission and was sent to the Officers' Training School in Bexhill.

"Please join me", he wrote. "We'll be able to have a few weeks together before I go overseas."

Early in our engagement I had had one of my presentiments — which I later found out was shared by Harry — that he would be wounded in trench warfare and would be sent home. But if he ever went back to France he would never return.

This thought haunted me. I handed in my resignation at the bank, and prepared to depart.

My last day at the bank was hectic, as a secret deal had been put through to sell the Wilson Shipping Line, owned by Lord Nunburnholme, a close friend of the late King Edward VII, to the Ellermans. That night the Wilson Line became the Ellerman Shipping Line.

We all had to stay till past midnight before the important deal was finalized. After that, in the early hours of the morning, the staff gave me a farewell party and presented me with a handsome cut-glass and silver salad bowl which I have to this day. It became a tradition that every Christmas morning Harry and I made a big fruit salad in this now over sixty-year-old treasure.

10
The Armistice

Harry duly received his commission as a lieutenant in the Canadian 31st Battalion, an infantry regiment which was earmarked to take reinforcements overseas. This would be his second trip to France after being wounded.

So once more on a forty-eight-hour leave we went north to stay with my parents in Hull. On

November 10, the day before my twenty-first birthday, we decided to celebrate. The party was to be a very joyous affair, but our hearts were heavy. I kept thinking of our foreboding about Harry's return, and the fact that he was being posted overseas for the second time.

The next morning, November 11, 1918, was misty, cold and grey. At nine o'clock our puffing little train was waiting for the guard's whistle. We had said our goodbyes through a heavy iron barrier, making us feel like prisoners on parole.

But shortly after we had taken our seats in the coach we were paged and called back to the barrier.

My father was waiting. He was very tense.

"I have heard a rumour," he whispered, "but we must not pin our hopes on it, that an armistice may be signed in a few hours."

You can imagine how light our steps and hearts were as we clambered back into the train.

There were only a few people in our compartment, two elderly ladies, a young clergyman and ourselves. At eleven o'clock our train pulled into Grantham station where we heard porters shouting and church bells pealing — what a welcome sound after four years of silence. A crowd was collecting. We alighted to hear that the Armistice had been signed. It was the best twenty-first birthday present anyone could ever have!

Back in the carriage we all smiled at each other, glowing with gratitude. The young curate asked shyly, "Would you mind if I offered up a prayer?"

It was an unforgettable moment as we all knelt to pray in the swiftly speeding Hull to London express. In later years it reminded me of a line from Noël Coward's *Cavalcade* "a strange heaven out of unbelievable hell."

When we arrived at King's Cross Station we

were surrounded by a huge mob. There was complete chaos. No one was acting normally. Taxicabs had more passengers on the top than inside. The milling crowds carried us along with them.

Food was out of the question. No one was working. Chefs and waitresses were singing and dancing outside the hotels.

Finally we got to the underground. That was worse, as the Cockneys in their pearly costumes and feathered hats were dancing the cake walk up and down the platforms. We would have liked to join in the celebrations, but we had to reach the camp at Bramshott that night, which we eventually did in a state of complete exhaustion.

There was a bit of a letdown as we stood in the rain while our landlady celebrated with her pals. She had waited for over four years for her husband to return. We felt sad when we thought of my grandmother in Hull sitting by her window looking for her missing son. But she was one of the thousands of wives and mothers who waited in vain.

So we hit the highs and lows on my historical, hysterical, never-to-be-forgotten twenty-first birthday, November 11, 1918.

After the Armistice the 31st Battalion was posted to a demobilization centre in Ripon, Yorkshire, where Harry was in charge of the officers' mess.

It was a riotous time as the troops, many of whom had just returned from the front, were very restless and anxious to get home. One night they decided to shoot off the spare ammunition. This spree caused much commotion, and was referred to by the locals as "the Ripon war".

I joined Harry in Ripon where we shared a house with Charles Knight, one of his fellow officers, his wife Etta, and Dorothy, their newly born daughter who was my godchild. They later met us in Canada and helped us during our first difficult weeks as immigrants.

Our old house in Ripon was cold and damp. None of us knew anything about babies, but I was always full of bright ideas — some of them practical!

"I know a warm place for her", I said. "Let's put her in a drawer by the kitchen range."

We had the sense to leave the drawer open, but when the district nurse called she was horrified.

"The child isn't getting enough air," she scolded. "You must have her in a cradle near the window."

Laundry was a problem. We put the baby's diapers to soak during the day, and when Charles came home from camp at night he helped with the washing, and either he or Harry hung it out in the yard. That was fine until a cow from the next plot chewed up a bunch of diapers!

No one in the district could make out who owned the baby, as first Charles would take her out in her perambulator and then Harry.

As we settled in we needed help as the house was so large. We managed to find a young girl named Eva who had spent all her working life in a dark cellar under some hotel, cleaning boots and doing the dirty work. I often thought of her in later years when we watched Ruby the scullery maid in the *Upstairs, Downstairs* television series.

Training Eva was some job. She suffered from acute catarrh and always cleaned her nose on the back of her hand and sleeve. But she was eager to learn. "Yers smarm, ow yers smarm" was her constant refrain.

At this time the men were hit by the golf bug. I was keen to join them and decided to practise my driving strokes in the living room. But after smashing the chandelier I realized I needed more territory.

Apart from the damage, Harry was delighted with my interest and took me to the golf course. I'm afraid we made a poor showing. Harry managed one very long drive but unfortunately hit a strolling cow in the udder. Its owner was furious.

On another occasion when Harry was swinging his club, missing the ball as usual, an old Yorkshireman standing by called out encouragingly " 'it the bugger agin lad!"

We enjoyed ourselves in Ripon, taking in the farewell parties and dances at the barracks. As the last men left the camp they auctioned off the silverware and linen. We bought some of the tablecloths which lasted us for many years.

We stayed in England longer than the rest of the troops as Harry was ordered to trace a sergeant who had absconded with the mess funds. He eventually found him in bed with a woman in Harrogate, but the wily sergeant managed to elude his captors before they could get him back to camp, and skipped to Canada with the money.

What a friend this man proved to be! He was never found, but the delay gave us six wonderful weeks in London on full pay, seeing the sights, attending tea dances and theatres.

Harry reported to Millbank every day, and then met me each morning at our rendezvous in Westminster Abbey.

"Has the sergeant turned up?"

"Not yet."

"Good. Where shall we go today?"

This was our real honeymoon, and we stored up many happy memories which were to help us through some of the tough and lonely times ahead.

11
Canada, Here We Come

Sailing orders arrived at last. Harry was looking forward to returning to Canada, and I was equally excited, with no inkling of what might lie ahead.

The parting from home and family was wet in more ways than one. The day of our departure it was pouring with rain, and, of course, we all wept. The family decided against going to Liverpool to see us off as it would be too upsetting. Anyway, we were only going for two years just to prove up the homestead. Our plans were to give Harry time to complete his work, and then return to England. So many of us had the same idea. Twenty years later when we made our first trip back to England we laughed and thought how easily we had fooled ourselves!

Harry was a quiet man, outwardly unmoved, but very sensitive. In order to make the long sea voyage easier on me, the night before we sailed he took me for a trip on the River Mersey to get my sea legs.

We boarded the dingy old troop carrier *Scandinavia* on October 10, 1919, and as soon as we got on board Harry said "We won't be sailing for another hour. Come down to the dining room and we'll have a meal first."

However, when we went back on deck I found the ship had pulled far away from shore, and so my thoughtful husband had spared me the pangs of watching my homeland disappear from sight.

We had a smooth crossing with several interesting travelling companions including some British parliamentarians who, full of optimism, were on their way to a peace conference. But to my dismay, the men and women were separated, and I had to share a cabin with three other war brides.

Probably because I was an only child I sometimes used to yell out in my sleep. The first night on board I dreamed my narrow bunk was a coffin, so I began screaming and scratching at the wall in an attempt to escape!

A young man dashed into our cabin, as his wife, one of my room mates, was expecting a baby. He thought her time had come!

It proved a terrible night — for all of us except Harry who was quartered in another part of the ship and slept peacefully throughout the uproar.

Being a city girl I was totally ignorant of pioneer life. Apart from what Harry had told me, which sounded quite unreal, my slim information had been gained from maps and movies. I remember shivering through one show watching mountains of snow, husky dogs and howling winds. My one thought was, "I must pack some extra sweaters" — or "jumpers" as we called them. So I arrived in Canada with more woollies than any Hollywood sweater girl ever dreamed of possessing!

Sailing up the St. Lawrence with the wonderful autumn colours was a sight I shall never forget. At last I planted my brogues firmly on Canadian soil and raised my eyes to a blue, blue Montreal sky. Then I felt very homesick and was acutely conscious of my stout English shoes when I saw the dainty footwear of the Montrealers. I was truly an immigrant!

But my spirits lifted after a scrumptious meal with real butter, and pie à la mode. This feast stood out as a highlight after our strict wartime rations. My soul was also fed by the brilliant colourings of the maples, the unforgettable vistas of reds, browns, and yellows, interspersed with the dark of the evergreens.

The train journey across Canada was indeed thrilling. I was intrigued by the tiny buildings, which to me looked like wooden kennels, peeping out every once in a while in this vast panorama.

I dashed out at the welcome stops, offering a handful of strange coins for purchases, always with one eye on the train. I never felt happy about leaving it, and was back in my seat before the call "All aboard".

I plied Harry with questions.

"What is Calgary really like?"

I hesitated to tell him that I always confused it with Calvary. But I was looking forward to the cowboys, rodeos, stampedes, Bob Edwards and his weekly paper, *The Eye Opener*, and, of course, the Rockies thrown in as a backdrop.

I pictured myself riding — my legs thrown over a sleek, shining horse, not under a massive bank ledger as they had been throughout the war years.

As I lay in the sleeper listening to the clanging of the train bell, my mind went back to the church bells at home. Tuneful and oh so sweet! This new bell was to be my bugle call, and still to me is the call of Canada.

In the middle of the night the train stopped with a sudden jerk, and the raucous cry "Calgary" was more alarming than exciting. Steam was rising from the engine, and our breath puffed out like tiny white clouds into the crisp night air. Although it was early October the snow had arrived early, and it proved to be one of the severest winters in southern Alberta for many years.

Then came a petrifying experience! As I stepped onto the platform I was grabbed and hugged by a huge brown bear! My heart stopped beating until I discovered it was our old friend Charlie Knight, who had come to meet us clad in his buffalo hide coat.

He bore us off to his igloo — which in truth was the top half of an old house, overpoweringly hot and airless for me, as I wasn't used to central heating.

It was marvellous to see Etta and her baby Dorothy again, and the four of us spent hours talking and making plans for the future.

That night Harry and I, balanced tortuously on a single cot bed, went to sleep with the clanging of the train bell ringing in our ears as a melancholy welcome.

12
Spilling the Milk

Our original plans were to head for the homestead as soon as possible. My idea of its location was hazy. I remember being asked by a Canadian in England, "Where is your husband's land?", and I replied, "At the foot of the Rockies." That was good for a laugh as he asked me which foot!

Harry had given me a graphic description of the little shack he had built. He assured me it had a good roof, real windows and a door which he had locked behind him when he left to join the army. He had taken his books, fur coat and guns over to a neighbour. Little did we know what it would look like when we eventually got there!

As he wanted me to get acclimatized to Canadian life before being plunged into the wilds, Harry suggested that we remain in the city for the winter and then go to the ranch of some friends of his near

Calgary. So we rented a small suite, our first home in the West, and chose odds and ends of furniture which would be suitable for our farm home later on.

Meanwhile Harry had to get a job. By this time the glamour of the returning war hero had disappeared, and ex-soldiers were left to struggle as best they could.

He heard of an opening in a railway office and, with his administrative experience and rapid shorthand, he confidently applied for the job. However, he was given a test on a typewriter with a broken key, and was rejected as unsuitable! A bitter pill to swallow after having given four years to his country.

So poor Harry was directed to the freight sheds where he did heavy manual labour until we left for the ranch.

It was a late spring, and the farmers had suffered greatly during the severe winter. They had lost many head of cattle, and it was a pitiful sight to see the skeletons of animals piled up against the fences where they had been driven in the blizzards.

Harry's friends, the Brauns, had a big spread which they managed for its millionaire owner. There was a large herd and hundreds of acres of crops. They were desperately short of help so they asked him if he would stay on and work for them for a while. We both thought this would be a splendid opportunity for me to learn how to be a farmer's wife.

But the Braun family didn't like me, and truthfully I didn't like them. I was summed up immediately as "green as grass. She don't know nothin'." This was true, but I learned fast.

One of my big disappointments was the fact that they had mislaid my precious mail. We'd been a week getting to the ranch from Calgary and I was desperate for news of home. Moreover, I'd once seen a mail bag disappear in the sea when being flung from the *Scandinavia* onto a tender on the St. Lawrence. One of my letters to my parents had been in that bag and I felt sure another bag had gone astray.

I wasn't at all reassured by the casualness of our welcome: "Oh, so you've come at last! We heard that a transport had gone down and we thought you two were on it."

My first friend was the Chinese cook, Wong. When I felt hopelessly down in the dumps he would comfort me, saying, "Don't worry, missie. I fix you nice Chinese food. Me homesick, too."

The old ranch house was large and rambling, and there were so many strange customs, such as the bed legs resting in cans of coal oil, as Wong explained, "Just to keep the bed bugs down, missie."

On the verandah stood a brand new piano in a crate. I asked more than once when they would bring it in but always received the same cryptic reply, "When Babe gets home. It's hers." So the piano remained outside and was a popular watering spot for the coyote hounds.

I was pathetically eager to help, but some of my attempts were heartbreaking. I watched Toots, the strong, stout young daughter, come in and toss a pail of foaming milk into the separator and turn the handle. It all looked so easy. So one day, when she put down the pail and was called away, I picked it up and attempted to toss it just as I had seen her do so often.

Alas, I slipped, missed the separator bowl, and the milk ran all over the floor. Wong came to my rescue and helped to mop it up. But my stock was very low that day. That's when I first heard the expression, "lower than a snake's belly".

Toots could also carry heavy sacks of flour and sugar, and I always felt she would have made good as a weight lifter in a carnival! But I gave up trying to copy her. Instead, I used to wander out alone and make friends with the animals.

"I would love to ride", I confided to Hank, one of the ranch hands who was very kind to me.

"Okay" he replied breezily. "Leave it to me, kid."

The next day he arrived with an Indian pony, a frostbitten, scruffy little cayuse, and led it into the corral. Fortunately Harry had bought a western saddle for me in Edmonton, so Hank threw this on the horse's back and hoisted me up. All I had ever ridden before was a donkey on the sands at Bridlington in Yorkshire!

I had no riding habit, and as it was a cold day Harry lent me his trenchcoat to wear over my dress. With this I donned a beret, and braced myself for what was to come.

Thank God there was a post on the saddle which I hung on to feverishly. The horse was mean and, with its frozen ears laid back, it took off at a gallop. But I managed to stick on, much to everyone's surprise, and was flushed with pride when Hank and the other boys said I was a "natural". They didn't say natural what!

My next adventure on horseback wasn't so successful. I mounted alone and planned to ride over the prairie, but the darned cayuse caught his foot in a gopher hole and threw me. Fortunately my feet slipped out of the stirrups, so the pony hi-tailed it for the corral and I was left to limp home.

But it was not long before Danny, as I christened my steed, and I made friends. He was my lifeline, and I spent many happy hours in the saddle roaming the lonely prairie — miles and miles with no house or human in sight. It was solace for the soul!

The vast expanse of ever-changing sky was always exciting, and inspired me to compose brief poems (not for publication) as I rode along. One of them, which I called *The Stampede Sky*, I recall to this day:

God's paint brush
Set the sky aglow
In far flung flames.
The tyranny of time
Diminished it
And calm night
descended.

The intercom in the ranch house was primitive, consisting of a grating in the living room ceiling that allowed the heat to ascend to the upper floor. All conversations floated up from the room beneath.

The chief broadcaster was the boss's wife who had a loud Yankee twang. One day when I was upstairs in my room writing my weekly letter home, Mrs. Braun, who was entertaining a visitor, broke through my concentration. She was obviously talking about me.

"She's one of them English war brides that's tooken our boys. City girl, too. Can't make bread even! As for milking, she don't know one end of a cow from t'other." (Udder would have been a more appropriate word!) "I've raised seven kids but none as dumb as this," and so on.

After hearing this recital through the grating, I tearfully pleaded with Harry to "get me out of this place".

I admit to crying a lot, but my tears froze either on the pillow or on my letters home. However, Harry's comforting words and his arms around me brought me to my senses. But for his love and understanding I would have bolted for home at that stage.

Harry spoke to the boss and it was arranged that as soon as the weather lifted we could move into a little cottage about a quarter of a mile away, which was temporarily empty.

Thank God time doesn't stand still! I spent the next few weeks happily cleaning the cottage, and moving day came at last.

We had sent to Calgary for our furniture which we had left in store, and with wedding gifts and "settlers' effects" we had enough to start with. My settlers' effects consisted of dozens of sweaters. Every time my mother thought about Canada she'd knit me a sweater, so I had enough to outfit a colony. But they made attractive cushions and I unravelled some for mats. I really became quite inventive.

This little shack was our first real home in Western Canada, and thanks to Eaton's catalogue — found you know where! — I fixed it up with chintz curtains and chair covers. It was really cosy and I began to relax at last.

13
My First Visitor

Spring arrived at last, and Harry was out all day driving an eight-horse team, harrowing or something. I'll say it was harrowing!

But I had Danny, the pony, a few chickens, and Buster, a black and white pup, half collie, half sheep dog, which had been given to me by a neighbouring rancher. Buster remained our constant companion and faithful friend for seventeen years.

But it was still a rather lonely life for me. Even Bossie, the cow, seemed to moo on a plaintive note. One day when she seemed particularly distressed I decided to milk her. So with pail, stool, and an optimistic stray cat at my heels, I took up my position.

It had looked so easy when Harry did it. I used to hear the swish, swish of the milk hitting the pail, and sometimes Harry would get an extra squirt from a teat and give the cats a lick. However, I didn't expect to do anything as spectacular as that!

So I settled myself in the correct milkmaid position. My first touch seemed to tickle her. She turned her head around and gave me a friendly grin, but not a drop of milk.

I then grabbed her firmly, but she kicked the pail over and knocked me off the stool. This made me more determined than ever. I must show who was the boss — me or Bossie! I pushed and shoved frantically, but there was no cooperation and no milk. I was evidently pushing the milk up into her udder instead of coaxing it down. Bossie stopped grinning and bellowed with anger.

I'd heard that cows like music, so I decided to sing *Home on the Range* which was all I could come up with at that time. Here we were out on the open range rendering a duet, Bossie moaning and me singing lustily! I was very excited when I heard a drop — but darn it all, it was rain not milk.

Next morning I was up early and watched Harry milk her with ease. I decided I would master the art or bust.

My second try was more successful. I managed to obtain a small stream of milk but it never seemed to hit the pail.

But after more practice I caught on and became quite an expert. Later, on the homestead, when we had thirty-two head of stock and five milk cows, I usually did the milking while Harry worked on the other endless chores. We accumulated this large scrub herd when homesteaders pulled out, leaving us their half-starved animals to feed. A very dubious asset, as we had to work twice as hard on the hay quarter to feed the hungry mob.

When we eventually returned to the city I always had a smile for the milkman who delivered our milk in sparkling clean bottles.

My first visitor called when I was sitting alone at my afternoon tea — a custom I found hard to give up.

There was a loud knock on the door. This threw me into a greater panic than any air raid siren ever did. The door burst open, and I knocked over my silver hot water jug. All I could see was a huge man with a bare, hairy chest and large navel.

"Have you seen a horse with a Lazy B?" he boomed. "I'm Tramp Blackson. Why, what's the matter, are you scared?"

I had no idea what he was talking about and was indeed terrified! There was my husband out with the horses and me alone with a Lazy B tramp!

But he laughed so heartily that I ended up laughing too and inviting him to tea. To see this hairy monster sitting at a daintily set tea table eating home-made muffins was an incongruous sight.

Mr. Blackson got very confidential over the tea-cups, giving me a few easy lessons on how to become a rancher's wife. His description of childbearing was graphic, and left me in a state of complete collapse. Never had I heard so many technical details!

"I've brought all mine into the world meself," he

boasted. He admitted his wife was in poor shape and I felt quite sick by the time he left. The fact that I thought I might be pregnant didn't help at all!

I learned later that Tramp was a close neighbour — at least two miles away which was close in those parts — and that he wouldn't harm a fly. All the same, I wouldn't trust him with my swatter!

Another unexpected visitor was a federal government inspector, Aubrey King, who had fallen in love with my bridesmaid in England, Hetty Alvin. She told me if he ever looked us up in Canada not to give him the slightest hope that she would ever marry him. But he was still confident that he could win her, and I had to lay it on the line firmly that his case was hopeless. He was nephew to King George's Librarian, and was able to give us an up-to-date account of London life. It was like a breath of fresh air to have a direct contact with my former world.

Aubrey still insisted on returning to England to change Hetty's mind, but he had no success and eventually died in the 'flu epidemic.

We spent many of our Sunday afternoons at neighbouring ranches where the private rodeos provided thrilling entertainment. These were real "ya-hoo" events where the cowboys broke broncos and practised for the big rodeos. Many of our cowboy friends became famous names on the international circuit.

But it wasn't all fun and games. One afternoon a tragedy occurred when a young rider was thrown and badly injured, after which he was confined to a wheel chair for life.

At branding time I was taken to the "dip" on the ranch where Harry worked. I was filled with horror as I watched the red-hot branding irons sizzling the hides of the animals, and it made me sick to hear the bawling of the young calves. But perhaps I wouldn't have been so affected had the cattle been our own! The brand used was HH, the name of the ranch owner, Harry Haynes. My husband's initials were the same, and we would indeed have been wealthy had all these cattle been our own.

At that time we had only one melancholy looking cow, a dog, three cats and a few chickens, while our boss, Harry Haynes, owned many hundreds of acres, and thousands of head of stock.

I felt very smart as I rode around the estate. My parents had sent me a discarded uniform worn by the "clippies", the wartime bus conductresses — navy blue with silver buttons. With my large hat, turned up at the side, I looked like a relic from Custer's last stand!

But I was still an ignoramus, and no one had thought to warn me about the devastating dust storms that suddenly whipped up out of nowhere. One day when I was pottering around outside the shack, I looked to the west and saw the angry black sky, with vivid streaks of red and orange. I scarcely had time to rush inside and slam the door before barrels, tools, and squawking chickens flew past the window. The boards on the frame shack loosened and shook, and the chimney pipe rattled.

What could I do? Terrified, I dashed to the bed, buried my head in a pillow, covered my ears and prayed. The racket was terrifying; I really thought the end of the world had come!

Suddenly the door burst open, and a tall, black man with round white eyes, like a Hallowe'en prankster, strode in. It was Harry who, forewarned about these prairie whip-ups, had provided himself with some goggles. He was unharmed, but his poor horses were not so lucky and were in a sad, battered state.

Later I learned the old prairie saying that a farmer only needed to sow every other acre, as the wind would blow the seed out of one field into the next.

14
The Camp Cooks

I had no time to be lonely that summer. Arthur Kilford, one of Harry's army buddies, wrote from Calgary to ask if he and his English bride, Hilda, could stay with us for a few weeks. They had just lost their first baby and Hilda had been very sick.

We were full of sympathy, and as they were going north with us later — Arthur was one of the four men who had filed a homestead claim — we had much to talk about.

Arthur was asked to stay on and help with the harvest, and we girls had time to talk and laugh over our strange experiences. We could hardly believe we were the same persons who had done war work in England — Hilda in a London post office, and I in a Hull bank.

One morning when our husbands were working in the field, the boss rode up in a frantic state to tell us his cook had left. All the harvesters would be going to the cook car that evening. He said he hadn't time to go to town for another cook and pleaded with us to help him out "just for a day or two, otherwise they will quit."

He knew we weren't used to cooking for twenty

hungry men, but asked us to do our best and he would be grateful.

Hilda and I had a hurried consultation, and as we could do with the money we decided we'd give it a try. Neither of us had any formal culinary training, but we did at least possess a cook book.

We found the cook car in a field. It looked like a long narrow garage on wheels.

We had been told the meat was in the back underneath the van, and that all the men wanted every day was meat, potatoes, vegetables and pies. Only the breakfasts differed — flapjacks, sausages, hashed potatoes, eggs, and, of course, porridge which they consumed in vast quantities.

We found the stove easily. You simply couldn't miss it. It was a big nasty piece of work which made the car hotter than hell when going full blast. I had added colour to my vocabulary by this time!

The ex-cook had left some meat in a big granite pot. It was a kind of sour stew buzzing with live and drowning flies.

"What shall we do with this lot?" Hilda asked.

"Throw it out", I replied.

"Do you mean the pot as well?"

"Certainly. We couldn't possibly clean that filthy mess."

So we started our first bit of pollution on the prairie.

Together we investigated the undercarriage of the cook car, and to our horror there was half a cow. Thank God it was dead! I'd begun to expect anything in this wild country.

"Whatever can we do with this?" Hilda asked.

"Help me pull the darned thing out and give me the saw. You go and make the pastry."

Hilda said she knew how to make pastry and I knew I didn't — at least not in quantity. So while she stoked the stove and made pies, I sawed away at the carcass. I've always had a respect for butchers after that introduction to their trade. What a ghastly way to earn a living!

Finally something had to give, and I broke through. Lugging the huge lump of meat into the car we found it was too big for the oven. So back to the saw!

Our first meal was a success — so the men said. They had been briefed to expect the worst from those two crazy English girls. But they treated us with respect, knowing that but for us they would have had to cook for themselves or go without.

After a week we wondered when the boss would produce the new cook. We were quite enjoying ourselves by this time, and when he asked if we would stay until after harvest time we readily agreed.

We began to get sick of the sameness of the menu and decided to give the boys a treat. I was good at making Yorkshire pudding, so one day we placed a large chunk on each plate. The idea was a flop! How can you introduce Yorkshire pudding to men from all parts of the world except England? After that we decided to keep to their regular fare, meat, potatoes and pies.

Our first batch of bread was a sorry sight. We knew nothing about baking bread in Canada or in any other country. We had picked up tips here and there and decided we were ready for it. But the bread turned out to be as hard as a rock — in fact a disgusting mess!

"What shall I do with it?" asked Hilda, who always sought my advice.

"Throw it in the pig pen after dark. The men will never know a thing about it, and the pigs will enjoy it."

There I was wrong. The next day the pigs were playing football with it and had no intention of eating it. Now I know it's not true when they say pigs will eat anything!

It was while we were camp cooks that we received some exciting news — not news of the second coming but it caused about as much commotion on the ranch. The owner of the estate, the millionaire, Harry Haynes, was coming to inspect the harvesting operation.

I was all of a dither as I'd never met a millionaire. Moreover, I never dreamed that he would come to the cook car. I figured he would have his meals served to him on a silver tray!

But, no, here he was in person. Hilda had gone for a quick nap, and I was having a much needed cup of tea. The half-gallon granite kettle was on the "hot as hell" stove, and I was wiping my perspiring brow when a long, sleek car pulled up, and out popped a short, fat man. I was fascinated to see him lift the steering wheel. It had been custom-made so he could tuck his plump tummy under the wheel without bending it. He breezily introduced himself as Harry Haynes.

"Do come in," I said politely as if I were inviting him into a drawingroom. "Would you like a cup of tea?"

Mr. Haynes readily accepted and sat down beside me on a long bench. As we chatted my shyness left me. After complimenting me on the tea, he invited me to visit him in Calgary as his wife was away and he was lonely. Fancy a millionaire being lonely, I thought.

But I felt quite sorry for him and when I jumped up quickly from the bench to grab the kettle for more tea — always comforting! — *bing*, the form seesawed, and my distinguished visitor was tossed into the air, crashing down the steps of the cook car on his backside. I must say he was a good sport and didn't fire me. He merely flicked "his" prairie dust off his sporty suit and returned for "another delicious cup of tea, please". I'd made an impression on him in more ways than one!

Hilda and I stuck with our cooking jobs until the harvesting was completed, which wound up with a farewell barn dance, another new experience!

15
Our First Heartbreak

By the time the harvest was in I was nearly six months pregnant, but being young and strong I stuck to my cook's job until the workers dispersed.

But I wasn't feeling too well and Harry insisted that I see a doctor. There were, of course, no prenatal clinics so we sought out the nearest doctor at Strathmore, a Dr. Giffen. After examining me he warned me there might be complications and he advised Harry to get me to a city where there would be proper medical and hospital facilities.

I wasn't too sorry to leave the ranch, and was much too happy thinking about the baby to have any regrets at leaving our little home.

We chose Edmonton as our stop-off. We decided that as soon as our infant was strong enough we would continue our travels — this time to our very own homestead which Harry had described so vividly.

As we knew no one in the city we looked through the phone book to find a doctor. Then I spotted the name Dr. C. U. Holmes.

"Look Harry," I said. "The same name as ours. I'll go and see him."

So I became a patient of Dr. Cecil Ulysses Holmes.

We were broke as usual, so Harry accepted the position of private secretary to Mr. Nelson, divisional superintendent of the Canadian National Railway. He very much enjoyed the job and often accompanied Mr. Nelson in his private railway coach.

We had found a temporary home for fifteen dollars a month on the upper floor of a small house on Jasper Avenue and 105th Street, now the business centre of Edmonton. At that time it was very primitive. We did have water laid on, but no electricity, and the coal-oil man called weekly with fuel for our lamps.

Plumbing was non-existent, and I pitied all the pregnant women like myself who had to waddle through the snow to the outhouse in sixty degrees below zero weather!

We were down to our last two dollars before Harry found his job. One day I handed him this precious money, giving him a list of what we needed and asking him to get what he could. My dear husband returned with a bottle of wine, a lobster, and a French loaf! Maybe he had the right idea. A feast is as good as a famine, so they say.

But we had two strokes of luck during our lean times. One day when Harry and I were out for a walk we found a big bag of groceries in the middle of the road, which had fallen off a wagon. A life saver for us!

On another occasion I went to the butchers and was standing at the counter next to a fur-coated lady who had bought expensive steaks, sweetbreads, and other delicacies which we hadn't tasted for so long. I, of course, had selected the cheapest cuts I could find, and not much at that. The butcher placed our purchases in our baskets and off we went. Imagine my delight when I arrived home with the steaks!

But despite our impecunious state and my condition, we spent a happy Christmas. We had been introduced to Bob and Emily Andison who were very kind and helpful, and remained our lifelong friends. Bob was Clerk of the Legislative Assembly at that time.

The highlight of those winter months was the opening of the Empire Theatre in Edmonton with *The Maid of the Mountains*. We had seen the show in London the year before. Little did we think we'd be seeing it again in Western Canada.

On a cold day in January, I was admitted to a private nursing home where I had a long and painful delivery. While I was still struggling to give birth, Dr. Holmes called my husband aside.

When he saw the doctor's face Harry knew something was desperately wrong.

"I can save either your wife or your child, but not both," he said gently.

So Harry sacrificed his little baby daughter for me.

It was a terrible time for both of us. In my desolation I pulled an invisible curtain around myself and emerged a changed person. I was now fully grown up and ready to face the unknown, whatever it might be.

As soon as I was out of the nursing home I plunged into the plans for our new life on the homestead. Bob and Emily Andison tried to dissuade us from going north, and Mr. Nelson was anxious for Harry not to resign. But Harry loved the land, and I would go wherever he went.

16
Home Sweet Home

So the die was cast, and we left Edmonton in the spring of 1921 on a mixed CNR train to Ashmont, and to a new phase in our lives.

We tossed and rolled around in the primitive railroad coach which pulled up with a jerk at every little hamlet to pick up livestock and farmers with their produce. The passengers were mostly Ukrainians until we arrived in the Ashmont district where many French Canadians and Metis joined us.

Ashmont was the end of steel, so here we had to arrange for someone to transport us by wagon and horse team on the rough Lac La Biche trail to St. Lina thirty miles north.

We had to stay overnight, and as the one small hotel was full a butcher and his wife offered us hospitality. But everywhere we went we caused quite a stir. We could almost hear their thoughts: "another green Englishman with a silly war bride going into the bush."

The federal government, out of the kindness of their hearts, had granted us another quarter section (one hundred and sixty acres). Quarter sections were thrown around with reckless abandon in those days. So with the sun and stars in our eyes, and our feet firmly planted in the gumbo, we started the next day on the trail to our new life.

After sitting all day, or one should say rolling, on a hard wagon seat with no springs, my enthusiasm was at a low ebb. I was sore in both body and spirit. The French Canadian who had come to meet us couldn't speak our language and we couldn't understand him.

Our destination was North West of 21, Township

62, Range 10, West of the 4th Meridian. But as far as I was concerned, our address might have been the North Pole!

I asked Harry how he ever found this remote place. He told me again of his hunting trip seven years before and how he had fallen in love with this part of the country. He also told me how another man had found his homestead. He and his wife, who were married in the United States, bought an old car to take them on their honeymoon. They decided wherever it broke down there they would settle. True to their word, they built on the spot where the old car gave up the ghost. It stood there old and rusty in their yard, but it had decided their fate.

I had a glowing picture of our new home ahead of us, and couldn't wait to get there. But to our horror and dismay, when we finally arrived there was no shack — just a heap of charred ruins. Everything of any use had been pilfered. Nothing was left, and our only welcome was the croaking of frogs and the buzzing of flies and mosquitoes.

About a mile back on the trail Harry had seen a deserted shack, so tired and depressed we had to backtrack to find shelter.

It was very dilapidated and dirty, and nailed to the door was a weatherbeaten note: HAVE GIVEN UP THE UNEQUAL STRUGGLE. HELP YOURSELF. What a sense of humour!

However it was the only shelter available and we had to move in. Our companion stayed overnight with his horse in a rickety adjoining barn.

We prepared our first meal on a rusty cook stove. Fortunately we had brought a good supply of groceries and, believe me, there was plenty of wood! In the years ahead we were often short of many things but never of wood.

I tried to be brave and calm and to accept all this

with aplomb, but we bedded down very deflated and unhappy.

Harry had brought yards of cheesecloth with him which I couldn't understand until the mosquitoes started their nightly raid. We slept under a mosquito bar as they loved our English blood! But we were so tired that we slept in spite of the nocturnal lullaby.

Suddenly I woke up screaming. "What is it?" The whole shack was rocking.

Harry, cool and calm as always, pulled me back under the blankets and holding me tight said quietly, "It's only a stray horse scratching himself on the corner of the shack." He knew instinctively the sights and sounds of this primitive country.

Awaking the following morning, after the gruelling shakeup on the wagon seat the day before, I was bewildered, scared, and stiff in every joint. "Where was I? Who was I? Why was I in a wooden box?" It was quite a time before I could answer myself, "You are on a homestead. You are Peggy Holmes, a war bride. The wooden box is your log shack."

The singing of birds, the croaking of frogs, the plaintive cry of loons on a nearby slough, the quacking of ducks returning north, and Buster barking all sounded like the *Dawn Chorus*. It should have been taped for posterity, but we had no tape recorders at that time.

The crackle of wood burning in the kitchen stove, and a welcome cup of tea brought to my bedside by Harry, my patient, unflappable husband, put everything back in focus.

Sitting up in bed, dressed in a beautiful but most unsuitable negligee for this part of the world, I pondered deeply. How long could I wear my fancy trousseau for my present way of life? Thank God, youth, energy and enthusiasm overcame my fore-boding.

After a quick splash and breakfast, we said good-bye to our companion, and took to the road ready to face the uncertain day. The sun was shining brilliantly. We felt this would be our lucky day and all would be well.

Ready to explore, with Buster bounding excitedly ahead, we viewed the shack where we had spent the night — from all points, north, south, west and east. It was built in a clearing and the Lac La Biche trail ran close by. The trail was an old one from Winnipeg, and was known as the Lac La Biche bull trail. There were no fences and light bush grew all around — tall, thin poplars and spruce trees.

It was good to fill our lungs with the pure pine-scented air. It was the first time I'd ever gone walking with a man swinging an axe. In this country one never went out without an axe; it would be like going out without your artificial leg, if you were an amputee.

My first lesson in the bush was to know how to find my way if lost. Perish the thought! However I finally learned to remember that moss grows on the north side of trees. I felt that this knowledge would lead me from one muskeg to the next and ultimately save my life.

During the day, a homesteader clattered into our clearing. He was driving a dejected, weary looking team of work horses hitched to a wagon full of settler's effects, with his saddle horse tied on behind.

As he spat out an evil looking wad of chewed tobacco, he announced curtly, "I'm on my way out. I've had it." Here was another human giving up the unequal struggle.

The resigning homesteader said he intended to sell the lot and suggested that we "do a deal". That's when we became real "wheeler-dealers". For Harry's custom-tailored London suit, his best shoes, plus a few dollars, we became the proud owners of a team of work horses, Nellie and Ginny — rechristened by us Skin and Grief — also the wagon full of junk and tools, bear traps, etc.

As a bonus the man said, "You can go over to my quarter and pick up anything you find there that you want." So we became real scavengers, and that's why, even today, it's difficult for me to pass a garbage dump without taking a good look around to see what people might have discarded.

Before leaving, this "outgoing" young man asked, "Lady, could you give me a hair cut?"

I agreed, and clipped away happily, first taking a swathe over the top. Never having graduated from barber school, and defying all union and labour laws by practising without a licence, I attacked his mop of hair with complete abandon. He seemed very happy with the cut, assessing it by the amount of hair on the ground and not by his appearance!

Harry said afterwards, "Good job he couldn't see the back of his head. It looked as if the mice had been chewing it."

Having shed himself of hair and all material possessions, the young man loped away in Harry's clothes — out of our lives and into his future. Looking at him as he faded away in the distance, I came to the conclusion that it's the man who makes the clothes, not the clothes that make the man!

Among the many things we learned was that when horses are left to graze, as our newly acquired team were of necessity, they tend to head back whence they came. Skin and Grief happened to be from South Dakota.

The first thing every morning Harry had to find these wandering horses and bring them back. We could not tie them up because we had no feed for them and they had to find their own. Buster was no help. He was a cattle dog. Cows he could round up but with horses he was no use at all.

While I was preparing breakfast, Harry was hiking after the horses, and the miles he tramped would have qualified him for the Olympic Games. What annoyed me was that he always returned so happy. I know he was glad to meet up with the nags. He would get some bearing on their whereabouts from settlers who shouted cheerfully, "They'll be another couple of miles or so by now." "Shouldn't wonder if they've made St. Lina this morning." St. Lina was five miles away!

Those darned horses always headed for the United States border. Sometimes I wondered if we flew the Stars and Stripes they might be induced to stay home. My idea was to get on and prove up, not waste time rounding up horses.

17
The Best Laid Plans

Our squatter's shack became the headquarters for Housing Development and Rural Planning — our nerve centre! We drew up yards of plans for the log house, barns, chickenhouse, pig pens, well site, vegetable garden, flower garden, fences, etc., burning the one and only oil lamp far into the night.

We both agreed that our log house had to be a home, not just a low building with a sod roof like most of the others. It must have two storeys with gables — custom built on a do-it-yourself basis. We both liked the idea of gables let into the roof to give style to the front. We hadn't a clue how to set about it, but hoped that supreme wisdom would descend from above and instruct us. A fully qualified architect with competent staff could not have been as prolific in turning out plans and specifications in such a short time.

It was indeed fortunate that we had found half a roll of building paper for our drawings. With these long rolls tied with binder twine, we stepped out like a couple of young executives, looking frightfully important. Only the odd squirrel and bush rabbit cocked their eyes as we passed by.

It was thrilling to be mobile. The pace was slow but who cared? The government had given us three years to prove up — six months residence per year — approximately ten acres of breaking and fencing the quarter section.

We had to build a barn, dig a well and put up chicken houses, etc. There were no building inspectors nosing around, and just imagine having all that dirt of your own to do as you liked on. It was beautiful black loam with a clay base. No fooling, it was the best in the west!

Number one on the list was to stake out the building site. There is an ancient saying, "A man should build a house, have a son and plant a tree". First things first — we would build the house. The son came many years later. And how ridiculous for us to plant a tree when we had thousands to be chopped down.

We decided to build our new home on the charred site of the old building. It would be a "Phoenix rising from the ashes." Even after fifty

Peggy at home in Hull in 1915, the year before her marriage.

Peggy and Lieut. Harry Holmes leave Liverpool for Canada on October 10, 1919.

Harry with the team, Skin and Grief, hauls logs out of the bush to build their house.

Above:
"The Gables", completed in 1922.

Left:
"The Gables" stands erect after 45 years, when Peggy and Harry, with their son and grandchildren, made a nostalgic visit.

Top left:
All Peggy's animals became pets. The pigs join a picnic.

Top right:
Peggy's unique riding attire—a London "Clippie's" uniform and long thick woollen stockings.

Above:
Peggy was the official barber in the bush. Here she is cutting the hair of a neighbouring homesteader.

Peggy and a neighbour saw logs for their wood pile.

Above:
Peggy and Harry complete their granary.

Left:
Buster keeps an eye on the livestock. The outhouse stands like a sentry box on the horizon.

years The Gables, as we had proudly christened it, stood solidly erect, the glassless windows staring westwards like a sightless old man — a house unwanted but undaunted.

A trip into St. Lina to buy necessities, and a tip-off that we could purchase some beef from a religious old crank who lived a few miles away, was an experience. After nearly breaking our jaws on the presumably fresh meat we bought from him, we found out later that the "holy" old devil had butchered his bull and was selling it to new settlers at baby-beef prices. We should have stayed with the rabbits!

Our immediate project was to put in a vegetable garden. We did just that and our crops yielded enough to feed a multitude. Secondly, we would snake out logs of uniform size for the building. This we did with our usual abandon, and fortunately snaked out enough tamarack to build and take logs to a small saw mill a few miles away. The lumber cuts were to make floors, doors, etc., and to do finishing jobs.

Thirdly, we would dig a well. I had no idea of being a diviner, but with native instinct and a willow wand I tuned in to the bowels of the earth. The pull near the building site knocked me over, hence my prediction, "Here's water and not too far down."

My first introduction to well digging was when we paid a visit to Charles and Etta Knight who had arrived at their homestead before us. On approaching their new lumber house I was surprised to see what appeared to be a small circus in the yard, with two men wearing coon-skin coats and panama hats, leading horses around a weird contraption in a constant circle.

Charles, who came to greet us, informed us they were the well drillers. We said hello to them and they continued their endless slow motion of going round and round.

Etta gave us a hearty welcome and we were pleased to see Dorothy again, their little daughter and my godchild. Etta had had time to experience some of the trials and tribulations of a home-steader's life, and it appeared that the well drillers were nearly driving her mad. They had come into their yard one day when the water supply was very low. Dorothy had to have pure water. Adults can take changes but not little children.

These men, after divining with willow wands, declared that they could get water at a very few feet, and at low cost. Unfortunately no contract was signed to that effect, and after the first few days of drilling it was evident that they were far below their original estimated depth.

Days after it was a case of — well, they have gone so far now, we may as well get to the water. But when they struck it at eighty-two feet, Harry and Charles together stopped them forcibly. It was far beyond a joke.

The cash which Charles had arrived with had been gradually disappearing, and this was the last straw. It was very hard for our friends to see these well drillers, after having been boarded and fed for over a week, ride off with Charles's pedigree stud horse in payment. Later we found the well was fill-ing up from about eight feet.

Etta told me she knew they had made a mistake coming into this wild country. Charles was a for-mer prairie rancher, but this was too rugged a life, building a house, digging a well, clearing the land, putting up fences, caring for stock, raising a child, and the endless chores that go with life in the bush.

When the Knights eventually left the district Etta

would never allow the word homestead to be mentioned. She wiped this experience entirely out of her life.

Despite this, we decided to begin digging our own well on the spot where I had predicted water would be found. With bucket and shovel, rope and pulley, plus our two pairs of hands, the first feet down were not too difficult. Harry threw up muck like an old gravedigger, and with his experiences digging trenches in the war he was soon out of sight below ground.

He next built a hangman's contraption for the pulley, and I as foreman-helper was instructed to haul up the full buckets of clay, empty them and return them to him. This may sound easy but try it, especially with a fifty-mile-an-hour gale to battle.

Harry called, "What's it like up there?" I replied, "Rotten. How's it with you?" His voice sounded weak and eerie. I didn't realize that he was slowly becoming asphyxiated and I could have been widowed at any moment. We lived so dangerously! I eventually retrieved him from what could have been his grave by heaving a heavy home-made ladder over the edge of the cribbing. Oh yes, we'd cribbed! Nothing came easy in this land of plenty.

Fortunately we struck water at twenty feet. We found out later that the water fissure ran in at about six feet. It was a slow one but gave us water for household use and watering the stock, filling up fitfully at its own peculiar slow pace. Had we dug deeper, I'm sure we would have hit natural gas. That would have been heaven and saved all the back-breaking work of sawing wood for heating. After our well-digging venture I feel sorry for all miners and people who work below ground — also their wives who wait above.

What a joy it was to drink the hard alkaline water

after the green slough water which was alive with wiggly worms. We must have been tough or we would have died of dysentry.

But to speak of dying was taboo. It cost a dollar a mile and ten dollars a visit for a doctor to come from the nearest point, which was thirty-five miles away. We couldn't afford forty-five dollars for that kind of treatment. We became, without knowing it, true Christian Scientists. Survival was entirely up to us. No rushing for antibiotics, pills or dope in those days.

18
Nostalgia

Once our well was in operation we decided to try to locate our hay quarter, which was three miles away from the home quarter. Just imagine Harry owning three hundred and twenty acres of land — especially after battling in France for a few feet of trench in mud-bloodied No Man's Land.

To get to the hay quarter posed quite a problem, but we had become first-class trouble-shooters and problem-solvers. The government had surveyed cut lines — every mile north and south, and every two miles east and west. Later, the cut lines were widened into road allowances. Where these cut lines intersected, a mound of earth had been erected, in the centre of which was an iron stake. Cut into these stakes were Roman numerals indicating the number of the quarter section to the southwest. So helpful — but not to me! Every so often there was a correction line, which completely threw out our calculations.

The trail was used only by hunters and trappers. No wagon had been through before. So now we were not only settlers but explorers — without a compass, except for the sun which had a hard time penetrating the dense bush.

As our wagon hit a tree with a jarring thud, Harry jumped out with his axe. He felled it — wham! Sweating and breathing heavily, he gasped, "We're opening up the road." I'd already figured that out, green as I appeared to be.

Progress was slow. We made about a mile a day. On our return journey the wagon jammed against the trees on the other side of the trail. I was thankful trails had only two sides. We never attempted traffic circles! A very jarring time was had by all. It was good that my teeth were strong or I would have broken both uppers and lowers, being so tense and apprehensive — always prepared for the worst.

After many backbreaking axing trips we reached our objective. Hillary couldn't have been as excited when he conquered Mount Everest for the Queen. We were doing all this for King George V and the Colonies, don't yer know!

We finally sighted an enormous meadow of soft, lush slough, which oldtimers assured us grew a heavy crop of Red Top hay. Personally I couldn't have cared less what colour the top of the hay was as long as it would provide feed and bedding for our cattle in embryo. Harry claimed it was the finest hay meadow he had ever seen.

There seemed to be no settlers between our quarters and the North Pole, at least we hadn't heard of any.

On our final day of discovery, Skin and Grief stopped suddenly and reared up on their hind legs in alarm. We didn't think they were capable of such a feat. Mind you, they didn't look anything like the white stallions of Vienna, the Lippizaners, even at this dashing angle!

Startled, we wondered what had caused them to panic. "Bears!" I cried. "No, there are no bears in this part of the country," Harry replied calmly. There he was dead wrong, which was proved later.

Suddenly, crashing through the bush, an apparition appeared — a giant of a man clad in white, with a long shock of red hair and flowing beard. He seemed to be on a chariot race, and was driving a team of oxen pulling him on a stoneboat, a long wooden box on runners used by homesteaders to clear the land.

He looked neither to right nor left but flashed past us as if he were Moses dashing back with his Ten Commandments. Or perhaps he was a visitor from outer space who had lost his saucer and had seized on the first thing he saw upon landing. We'll never know. It was unnerving, but we were learning to take everything in our stride!

Shortly after this episode Harry decided to go over to the Vanderveer's place, five miles from our homestead, where he had left a trunk containing his books, fur coat and shotgun when he went off to the war.

It was a lovely day — cold and clear. The trees and countryside were covered in hoar frost. It was a fairyland! Breathing in the pure, clear air — yes, the air was pure in those days — we sat side by side on the hard wagon seat. Skin and Grief, our odd plug team, plodded along relaxed in every way, particularly their bowels, as they happily fertilized the earth along the trail. Diapers for horses had never been heard of in the early 1920s.

James Vanderveer, an American college football

hero, had been one of the trio with Harry when they staked their claims. He and his wife, Bessie, had stayed on the homestead with their children, cattle and chickens until the Americans entered the war. James then decided to return to the United States to enlist in the army, but tragically for the little family he died on the way out with 'flu.

So I was prepared for an empty house, but when we drove into the deserted homestead a cold chill enveloped me. There stood a once beautiful two-storey home, with broken windows and sagging door. It made me think of *Wuthering Heights* and the Brontë country.

I followed Harry into the dark, damp main room which was like a tomb. It was obvious that the Vanderveer family had made a hurried departure. Possibly James had already developed the 'flu and was anxious to get away. A few mugs and plates were still on the table, and birds and cats had obviously been lurking there.

I stayed close to Harry as we went up the stairs to the upper floor. The low ceiling was festooned with cobwebs which hung like gossamer curtains. Unseen eyes were watching us — probably only mice — but I knew the house was haunted, if not by ghosts by too many memories of the past.

Remnants of tattered bedding lay on the mouldy mattress where cats had bedded down. A child's crib had been used by birds as a nesting box. In another room by a small bunk lay a child's nightgown, a few articles of clothing, plus some dead birds.

I was choked with emotion — such a lovely home gone to waste!

"Let's get out of here quickly", I pleaded.

Harry searched around until he found his box of precious books, among them *Palgrave's Golden Treasury, Pilgrim's Progress,* and the works of William

Shakespeare. The edges had been chewed by mice, evidently bent on digesting knowledge. They appear to have favoured the *Golden Treasury*, but Harry and I made a leather cover for it, and it is still on my bookshelf.

The shotgun was there but in bad shape, also the fur coat, the most moth-eaten garment I've ever seen. I've no idea what kind of animal it came from!

Harry and I looked out of the broken window onto the neglected yard below. There, close to an overgrown bush, were two little crosses marking the graves of two of their children. What a tragic sight! I began to sob uncontrollably — in fact I wept all the way home, clutching the filthy old fur coat which I refused to have draped over me.

"I can't bear it near me", I told Harry. Little did I think, when the weather dipped to sixty degrees below zero, that I would be glad of it.

This was our first day off since signing away our lives to prove up. You paid the Government of Canada ten dollars and they bet you'd never stay the course!

As we approached our shack we could hear our assorted herd of scrubs howling for us to get cracking and throw them some feed. The milk cows were mooing for relief of their udders as it was long past milking time.

My spirits revived somewhat as I pitched hay to the cattle and watched Harry, with his head tucked into the side of Lola, our only milk cow at that time. The smell of fresh milk, and the warmth of the old log barn gave me courage to face our next adventure, or should I say misadventure.

19
A Haying We Will Go

Breaking was next on our list. With a borrowed six-teen-inch walking breaker plough we set out with Skin and Grief, Buster the dog, our lunch and an alarm clock.

The patch of land was cleared except for stumps and rocks. How delightful it was to see the dark earth turn over, looking just like chocolate bars. Every time we hit a stump or rock, which was fre-quently, one or other of the plough handles would give us a dig in the ribs, hard enough to knock me off my feet. Prizefighters get big money for less punishment.

The alarm clock, which we called the Town Hall Clock, was placed at the top of the row and was set for noon when we planned to stop for lunch. Stones had to be carried away. That was my job. Stumps had to be dug out which was tackled by Harry. How we would have welcomed some of today's modern equipment!

At the end of a long hard day we wearily wended our way homeward to the eternal rabbit stew — by candlelight — which some might think romantic. But it was merely because our oil had run out.

Buster had taken off overnight on what we thought was one of his hunting trips. So next day we returned to our backbreaking task without him. When we reached the plough we found Harry's coat which he'd taken off during the heat of the day and forgotten it. There was Buster guarding it. He'd been there all night. How's that for loyalty?

We had very little time for visiting, but we man-aged to get together occasionally with a few of our former army friends — settlers such as Hilda and

Arthur Kilford who had visited us on the ranch the previous year. They had brought our household effects along with their own in a railroad car, and transported them by road for thirty-five miles where they stored them in one of their sheds so we could get them as soon as our house was built.

The Kilfords were also working desperately hard to get established. It was every man for himself, working against time.

With the proceeds from the sale of my piano in England we had some cash in our pockets and were at last able to buy another milk cow. We had heard that Mr. Lesage, a French Canadian near St. Lina, had stock for sale.

So we took a day off to make this most important purchase. We found our man quite easily, but our attempts at a business transaction were hilarious as we had difficulty understanding each other. But I did understand, and was slightly shocked, when I heard him allude to his son as "a cute leetle bugger". Harry assured me he wasn't swearing but I wasn't used to such endearments at that stage in my life!

Mr. Lesage insisted on taking us to meet his family, and business seemed to be the last thing he wanted to discuss. So we were introduced to his smiling wife, Madeleine, and their long lineup of children.

The hours went by as we consumed vast quantities of food, and sampled the brew which was just ready. Finally Harry came to the point.

"How about selling us a cow?"

Mr. Lesage then trotted out a little brown and white milk cow called Blanchette. She was cute, with beautiful brown eyes, and we fell for her. Blanchette also had an attractive calf named Toto, and we felt we just couldn't part mother and son.

Just then a strange creature hove into sight. She

was grey and black with crumpled hoofs that turned up like gondoliers' slippers. She had no ears — her hoofs and ears had been frozen. This was Croquette, the mother of Blanchette. A good milker in her day, the owner told me, but she had frozen teats too.

It was like a three-ring circus. Mr. Lesage swore, "I'm going to kill that old crooked one!"

My heart was tender and I couldn't bear the thought. Stupid as I was, it never dawned on me that it was beef and they could eat it. I pleaded with Mr. Lesage to save her life.

"No", he announced firmly. "I'll kill her for sure."

Knowing nothing about stock I exclaimed, "Oh Harry, do let's buy her. It's such a pity to split up the family."

So we settled Croquette's fate and bought the whole French bovine family. Bang went all my piano money!

We drove home with the old crooked grandma, the dainty milk cow, and the calf frisking by their side. Buster was delighted as he could return to cattle herding for which he had been trained on the ranch.

What a cavalcade! The tiger lilies were nodding a friendly greeting by the roadside. The ripening grain nodded and waved gaily, whispering, "So you've given up your music and become a milk-maid."

We had also purchased some chickens and sacks of feed. So that was the day we went into mixed farming on the proceeds of a piano.

On arriving home Harry started to unload when he discovered two sacks of feed were missing. This was more than we could afford to ignore, so he had to go back to see if he could find them.

A few miles away he spotted the two sacks on

the top of a hill in the middle of the road, with our faithful Buster mounting guard. Some neighbours told us later that they knew the sacks were ours because they saw our dog. They wanted to bring them to us but, oh no, just try to pick up something of ours while Buster was in charge.

But now we had fresh milk, and with a dash churn I was able to produce some fairly good butter. It would never have taken a prize. In fact I had a hard time coaxing the storekeeper to take it in trade — even at ten cents a pound. But we enjoyed it.

With our rapidly growing herd we had to face the problem of winter feed and shelter for all of us.

We also had to get down to haying, and this was going to be too big a job for the two of us. So when a family a few miles north, Earl and Maisie Morris, formerly from Missouri, appeared on the scene with an offer to help us on a crop-share basis, we grabbed the opportunity. Help of any kind was sent by God, especially when we didn't have to part with cash.

The mud holes on the trail to the hay quarter had not dried up when we set out, and the going was very treacherous. Maisie, a fat jolly women, sat beside me on our wagon.

Noticing my bruises she realized how hard this mode of travel was on me. I hadn't learned to roll around like a sack of potatoes as the others did.

"Say, why does you sit so stiff?" she asked. "When you sees a bump a'comin', go soft like I do."

So she taught me how to relax, for which I was ever grateful to her. I was just learning this new motion when slop, slosh, splash! The horses and wagon were bang in the middle of a mud hole. No amount of "gettie uppie" would work. There we were, firmly embedded and sinking all the time.

This is where Earl Morris came in handy. He claimed to have been in tougher spots in Missouri. His team pulled ours out, then when his team stuck he called for us to pull out "hissen's".

When we reached the hay quarter our first task was to erect tents, as our plan was to camp while putting up the hay. We managed to cut hay for half a day before it started to rain steadily and heavily for nearly a week — enough to float the Ark. We remained under canvas in the water-logged camp, praying to the Lord to send a dove down from above. He must have heard us because the weather dried up suddenly.

Maisie did the cooking as I preferred to work in the hayfield. She was an expert at whipping up a stack of pancakes under the most adverse conditions, and prepared some quite tasty dishes, except for the special which she served one day, proudly announcing it was squirrel stew. It smelt delicious and they all tucked into it with gusto, but as the poor squirrels' relatives were playing in the trees overhead, I couldn't touch it.

A rippling creek ran through the middle of our hay meadow which was connected by a rickety corduroy bridge thrown over it by a settler some years previously.

Eyeing it dubiously I was sure it wasn't safe. "It's rotten. It won't hold a load," I announced firmly.

But I was told that the bridge had been up for a long while and I was always looking for trouble. There was no time to stop and build a new one now.

We completed the mowing after the rain ceased and the grass had dried. But there had been too many delays and our nerves were getting frayed.

My job was raking with the team, wielding an enormous hay rake, tripping it and making lovely long rolls. The smell was heady. One can enter another dimension just by smelling hay — no need to sniff glue!

I then piled the hay into windrows. It was all very hard work. We seemed to have a passion for doing everything the hard way, and ever since this homesteading stunt I've become a short-cutter. If there's an easy way around a problem, that's the one I take.

Eventually we were ready to drive the wagon over the bridge to get our first load of Red Top. Much to my surprise we made it. I could see the grins of my companions!

We were at this time expecting a blessed event as Grief was in foal. Skin and Grief were given the dubious honour of hauling the first loaded hay rack across the bridge.

Pitchfork in hand, I stood atop the load like Nelson at Trafalgar. Then it happened just as I had predicted. The horses stepped onto the bridge, digging their hooves into the poles and tearing them apart. Down they went, hanging pathetically on the stringers by their bellies, kicking their legs in a swimming motion, getting nowhere of course as they were strung up above the water.

I yelled bloody murder, and as the rack turned over I made a flying leap, jumping clear just in time.

This was a day of disaster. Grief lost her foal. Hay was strewn all over the place. I was bruised and ready to be taken to a mental hospital in a straitjacket. Earl and Maisie coped alone for a while while Harry calmed me down. As he said, "It could have been worse."

As the rains had held up work, the Morris's had

to return to their own place before the last stack was finished. The last straw — this was it!

We had been loading and stacking all day and were tired out. It was a beautiful evening so we decided to call a halt and top off the stack the next day. We would take a chance and leave it open for the night.

After our meal we sat snugly and smugly for a while, then bedded down early as we were both dead tired. At two a.m. a clap of thunder rocked us into a sitting position. Another clap, and vivid fork lightning.

"Peggy, get up", Harry shouted. "We'll have to top the open stack before the rain comes or the lot will rot."

Quick as fireman answering a three-ring call, we were on the job. Harry was on the hay rack pitching the hay up to me. I worked like the sorcerer's apprentice! Every time the lightning zig-zagged across the black sky, I threw down my pitchfork. I had no intention of acting as a lightning conductor to save a stack of hay.

But my work was to top the stack and I couldn't run away. The storm was right overhead and was the worst I've ever experienced, although I've never again been on the top of a haystack in the middle of the night with a raging electric storm all around me.

We did eventually finish the job, congratulating each other on getting it done before the deluge. The fact that it never rained at all was something we never referred to. Murders have been committed for less!

So our haying ended, and on bended knees we thanked the Lord.

20
Meeting the Neighbours

We had a colourful assortment of neighbours, although we were too busy for much visiting. One family intrigued me — Mr. and Mrs. Wilbur Keltie from Kentucky. Mrs. K., as she was always known, was lean and scrawny, and had a quick, direct approach like an inquisitive bird.

Our first visit to them was to buy some chickens and vegetables which they grew in profusion. As we drew up at the log cabin, out loped Mrs. K., calling, "Light and let's look at yer seat."

I was stumped by this remark until Harry said, "I think she means for you to get down and go in." Thank heavens he was there to interpret or I would have looked a complete fool!

Down on terra firma Mrs. K. bade me enter. A few cats streaked out of the door as I groped my way into the dark room. I was just about to sit down when Mrs. K. yelled, "Mind yon cellar flap. It's none too safe." As I was about to seat myself right over the trap door I made a very fast move.

There was only one room for the whole family. Knowing the couple had several children I tried to picture them all together. Where did they sleep? And where did they bathe? But Harry told me they probably washed when the river broke up in the spring.

"Would yer like to slake yer thirst?" Mrs. K. asked.

Very timidly I replied, "Yes", wondering what brew they whipped up for guests.

"Well, help yerself. There's bucket and dipper. I'll cut yer a slice of 'rootbeggar'."

Rutabaga is a kind of Swedish turnip which, where I came from, they fed to the stock. It was a primitive snack but offered from the heart. Speaking of heart, this combination of turnip and water lingered around mine for hours.

Hearing a wheezing sound coming from behind the enormous cook stove I wondered what on earth she was cooking. But Mrs. K. enlightened me. "That's my youngest kid, Walter," she said. "He's got a bad chest."

She coaxed him to "come on out and see the lady". Not on your life! He didn't want to leave his iron lung. She dragged him out yelling bloody murder.

The poor child was a revolting sight. He was fat and podgy with congested lungs to the point of pneumonia, and mucus pouring from both nostrils. A sick feeling overcame me.

Walter always had his jacket buttoned down the back. I asked Mrs. K. why he wore it back to front, and she explained, "Well, it keeps his chest warm." This was somewhat illogical as his back was bare!

The conversation was definitely afternoon tea-ish. Mrs. K. discussed the neighbours, and was especially interested in the new settlers.

"Now take that English woman, Mrs. Bright," she said, "with her fine airs and fancy talk, spiking around on them high heels. She'll stick in the mud for sure."

How right she was, and so full of earthy wisdom.

"Now when I buy shoes, which ain't often," she added, "I go to the store, sit and say, fit me. No nonsense! And when they fit I says, now bring me two sizes larger. Never did have no corns nor bunions, and never did have trouble with *my* feet!"

Becoming conscious of mine, I tucked them under the backless kitchen chair and hoped she wouldn't think them unsuitable.

So ended my first afternoon tea at the neighbours.

On the way home I asked Harry if he knew how many children they had. He thought six.

"Do they all live in the one room?" I asked.

"Yes, I suppose so in the wintertime", he replied, "but sometimes in the summer they may bed down in the barn."

I thought how little need there was for sex education in the St. Lina district school. They received it in the home and in the barnyard.

On later visits, Mrs. K. talked like a waterfall hell-bent to the sea. She explained that she had had "little schoolin' " and to reach her Kentucky school, "I just had to go down one mountain, up another, round a bend and I was there. That was if the weather was good and after I'd milked four cows."

All this made me realize what hardships these people had to endure. To me Mrs. K. was a graduate from Hillbilly College, Kentucky, with native knowledge and accomplishments that would have put a Ph.D to shame.

Continuing her reminiscences in a hard, nasal monotone, Mrs. K. confessed, "I never did read a novel till I was thirty-six years old."

After that, she apparently lapped them up, and was an avid reader, thriving romantically on *True Story* magazine, and hot lurid romances.

Mrs. K. was also a self-taught herbalist, using her sixth sense or native intelligence. "If the herb don't work, you do," she would say. So if the patient died, you knew it was the wrong remedy. Pretty much on par with today's drug scene!

"Never did believe in too much water," she said.

"Now, take that Englishwoman, Mrs. Bright. She bathes her kid every day. Ain't no good at all to do that. She'll rub off all the kid's light skin, it being as thin as paper anyway. The poor little devil sure looks weak. Now, take my kids — fat as hogs. I rub fat into 'em."

But her fat applications didn't seem to have oiled their respiratory organs. They all wheezed like sat-on concertinas.

Dental care was, of course, unheard of, and Mrs. K. envied the coyotes' teeth. Every time the hunters brought them in for skinning, she would examine their teeth and ruefully feel her one and only front fang which, as she said, was "good enough to spike an onion."

I shuddered at the description of her extractions. "Some just rotted," she said, "and with a bit of string and a nail on the door, I slammed the door shut meself — never did hit a dentist's chair. Tough, aching ones — well, I hitched the team, went to the store, sat down on a stool and said to the storekeeper — pull 'em out. Never did have no pain killer."

The thought of dentures never entered the minds of the settlers. What little money they had they needed for their farms. Their thrift was amazing. They would keep a smudge going outside to save matches, and would go to bed early to save coal oil.

Should a visitor drop in, someone would sit by the lamp and turn up the wick just enough to see by. Tea was made from the dried bark of spruce trees. Coffee was roasted wheat, and medicine came from the woods — herb and peppermint tea. But survive they did — at least some of them.

Despite their poverty they were very big-hearted and would always lend an implement or a hand when necessary.

Surprisingly enough, most of them kept their sense of humour. I remember one man from Virginia, who always had a big grin. He worked for various farmers and prided himself on never failing to have a good joke handy for his employer.

One day his wit deserted him and, while he was milking, no joke would come. He sat in the barn worrying over this, when he had a brainwave. In his own words, "I opened the door and threw my hat at the lamp." This he claimed brought the house down.

"In flames?" I asked. But that was definitely over his head!

21
Moving In

With the approach of fall, we felt it would be wise to finish building on our home quarter before freeze-up. This travelling every day before we could begin work on the house was too exhausting.

While Harry was building pole corrals and shelter for stock, I was peeling logs — wonderfully healthy work and all one needs to keep fit. Far better than a mechanical device in a silhouette parlour.

With a two-handled drawknife you sit astride a log and peel off its bark. You have to keep rolling the logs. But it is satisfying work and you can see the results of your labours. Nice clean logs ready to build our home.

A dug-out cellar under the house was necessary to keep our precious vegetables and potatoes, otherwise they would freeze. If we'd only known about deep freezing food. We only knew that you could freeze meat, fish — and ourselves. The rest of the frozen food we threw out. The locals warned us that if a can of food got frozen it must be destroyed as it was poisonous.

Building measurements had to be carefully planned, and all logs sawn to a uniform size. Harry did this work with a one-man cross-cut saw, chopping the corners with an axe. He was a terrific axe man. Even later, when we lived in the city, he'd grab an axe to do any little finishing job around the house, and we always kept one at the front door to chop away the ice on the inside before we could let friends into our jerry-built war-time home. I suppose you would call him a rough carpenter!

The first few rounds were not too hard for us to handle, and the corners fitted perfectly. The building was twenty-six feet long and fourteen feet wide. Each day it was a thrill to see the walls rise, solid as the Walls of Jericho. No trumpets could have budged this lot!

But it was getting harder to handle as we went higher. We had to invest in rope, lots of it, enough to go under a log and over the wall, with me on the other side of the building driving Skin and Grief which were hooked on to the ropes. Harry would yell to me, "Git up" and, "Whoa", and guide the log into its place.

We became extremely ingenious and stuck at "nowt" as we'd say in Yorkshire. But windows and door cuts were trouble spots. When I see the pre-fabs being thrown up today, my mind goes back to our backaching times.

Other settlers were doing the same thing, each in his individual style. Most of them were more sensible than we were and didn't attempt such large structures. They knew the country better and figured a small, low place would take less fuel, hold the heat longer, and be more comfortable in the winter time.

The logs were now ten rounds high. That would be the first floor. We knew it would be humanly impossible to finish the upstairs before winter, as it was by then the end of October.

Our "think tank" went into action for a night session. No light in the dome, just an oil lamp in the window! We had to come up with an idea which eventually dawned with the daylight. We would put down the sub-floor with rough planks, and board the ceiling in. This could later form the floor of the second storey. We would camp inside this cosy enclosure until warmer weather would allow us to build higher. So we laid the floor as quickly as possible, much to the detriment of our knees. Housemaid's knee is painful, and we both had it!

During the summer we had added extensively to our possessions, mostly from homesteaders going out. More were going out at that time than coming in. They would leave us a couple of cows if we would feed them. They also threw in some chickens and cats. We agreed to give them a cow on their return. But most of them departed for ever.

One man left us a beautiful saddle horse — another Frenchie named Mignon — in return for enough cash to get him to town. Mignon was my pet, my pride and joy.

I cut this man's hair for free too, as a haircut was thrown in with every deal. As I clipped away and sang, the Barber of Seville must have turned green with envy. I had many customers, most of whom were going out to "make a poke". But they never came back. No doubt they lost their poke in a game of poker, or were sandbagged by four aces!

We became swamped with stock and other cast-offs. Our shack was a salvation centre, not so much soul saving as life saving!

Our howling herd had to be fed, watered, and most of them milked. Those fellows had known we had plenty of hay — that's why they picked us out. Just like the give-away deals so prevalent today. All had strings attached (ours had udders) and we had a milking problem.

Chores were mounting daily. Sometimes I felt that God should have given us more than two hands when he had given a cow four teats.

We whipped up temporary shelters for chickens, and a log barn which was a gift from another desperate character on his way out. These logs were numbered and hauled over, and now became "our barn". We threw poles across the logs and piled straw high on top. Hopefully the heat of their own bodies would be sufficient to keep the stock warm all winter. We lived on hope and rabbits!

Our furniture was retrieved from its crude storage with the Kilfords. It was a joyful occasion to meet up with it again. Kitchen cabinet, Morris chair, homesteader kitchen cook stove, tin heater — all are now Canadiana items and would bring high prices.

We also got our beds, linens, blankets, wedding presents, and our precious Royal Doulton dinner and tea service, a setting for eight, our silver tea service, rugs, cretonne for drapes and cushions, table and chairs, plus an indoor chemical toilet — for me only, as the men used the barn.

There was also a gramophone, the kind you wind up with a handle, and two records — Bettina Freeman singing *Knowest Thou the Land* — so appropriate — and the *Anvil Chorus* which I cannot tolerate. The "clang-clang-clang of the anvil" reminds me of Harry. As I looked through our small north window, there he was silhouetted in the moonlight, even when it was below zero. He was musically sawing logs to be devoured during the night by our ever-hungry stove, with not a log remaining by breakfast time.

We had no efficient furniture men to drive up to the door, to handle and wrap our precious pottery and put padded covers around our furniture. We had to lift the darn things ourselves, clean off the straw and muck, finally heaving them into the wagon box while Skin and Grief leaned in their traces wondering what in the name of God we were up to now.

It was a perfect Indian summer until the first week in November — that was our Exodus. But we were on the move at last.

Cattle, chickens and all livestock were moved first, then the furniture was dumped. We decided upon a ceremonial entry onto our very own land. The moon was high in the sky on November fifth (Guy Fawkes night) — a suitable date. Now I know the joy of a moonlight flit!

We chose to ride bareback on Skin and Grief as they had been so faithful. I led Mignon, my saddle horse, with our good friend, Buster, bounding ahead.

When I say we rode bareback, don't get the idea that I did the Lady Godiva act! But we looked like biblical characters — sort of is-there-room-at-the-inn types.

22
Chinking

We were in our own home at last. Only the straw to throw on top of the ceiling and to chink between the holes in the logs. Without chinking, our building looked like Fort Edmonton. We could have defended ourselves by putting our guns through the gaps in the walls.

The good weather ended two days after moving in, and winter clamped right down on us. We got colder and colder, also larger and larger as we donned extra clothing. That was my first introduction to the Stanfield family. Stanfield underwear was a must, and no settler worth his salt would think of homesteading in any other kind. I later voted for Mr. Bob Stanfield, when he was leader of the Progressive Conservative party, mainly on account of his underwear! We could not possibly have existed throughout the winter in those conditions without every inch of our bodies being covered.

Then we thought of the tent. That was the answer! We would put it up inside our four walls. Surely we could beat the cold that way. So that winter we were under canvas — a home within a home.

But even in the tent we were frozen and our blood literally congealed. Our circulation and our spirits hit zero. Crying to God was no use. Something had to be done.

Harry pleaded with me to let him crate the chickens. "Could they spend the night with us?" he asked.

I sternly refused, but when I thought of those

poor hens laying frozen eggs, I capitulated. "Nail them down and bring them in!" I said.

What a night! We were dog tired, and slept despite our troubles. But those ruddy chickens somehow managed to get out of the crate. Delighted to be warm and free, they disported themselves on the kitchen cabinet and the top of the stove, clucked and fussed happily, and one laid her egg on the table.

We eventually caught them, nailed them down again, and took them some miles away to a neighbour to board them out for the winter and so save their lives.

The chosen chicken keepers were the Sergonnes, a kind and understanding couple, who said they would look after them and give us a couple of roosters for our Christmas dinner.

Apart from the relief of getting our chickens looked after, this visit didn't lift my spirits at all. Mrs. Sergonne had been a school teacher and had married a farmer. She was "bushed", had let herself go, and was hopelessly depressed.

Her opening remark was, "Move your chair from the wall. The bed bugs are very bad — I can't keep them down." I did some fast footwork.

She pulled on a cigarette that hung loosely in her sagging mouth. "Take advice from me girl. Get out before it gets you!"

It was no use sobbing all the way home. The tears would have frozen on my face.

The trip home was majestically beautiful, through a large spruce bluff wearing a heavy, fresh coat of snow. I can understand how Reggie Morris, an artist friend of ours who came out from Wales, felt about the setting. His wife had to drag him in with frozen fingers and thaw him out, but he painted some marvellous winter scenes.

The splendour of it all inspired me to verse, as I

hadn't started to paint at that time. I got down to that when I was sixty! I remember one of my unstructured efforts which I called *Indian Prayer*:

The rising sun
Guarded by sun dogs
In the eastern sky;
Rainbow colours casting golden glow
On pure white snow.

The old bull trail hidden,
Parka fur frosted
From icicles on nose.
Moccasined feet
Numbed with cold.

Teepee smoke
Miraged over endless white.
Great God, give me strength,
Having travelled far
So near to journey's end
To reach sun dogs and home.

Our chores were endless. As we neared home we could hear the cattle bellowing for food and water. The next day the well froze. This was double disaster. The lake was frozen so it was no good taking the herd there. Tubs and buckets had to be filled with snow and put on the cook stove to melt. All day long this life line had to be kept flowing, and you get precious little water from a large tub of snow. The first cow was mooing for more water by the time the last one had received her quota late in the day.

The "think tank" then came up with a bright idea. We would put a lighted lantern down the well, and cover the top with blankets. That did the trick. Only a trickle of water got through, but the steady flow saved us endless work.

During this time I was getting mail from home telling me about the family parties, theatres, etc.

Still suffering from homesickness these letters did lttle to comfort me. My parents asked me to describe our home. All I could tell them was, "Well, it's something like Selfridges' roof garden and the Hull Pier, with a flat top."

A friend from my banking days in Hull kept me posted with news of England, and I replied with a blow by blow of our life. An elderly uncle of hers travelled from Bridlington to Hull once a month to hear the latest from "that daft lass in Canada."

It wasn't long before the hay we had brought from our haying trip ran out. Harry had to go all the way to the hay quarter, fence the stacks and bring back a load, while I stayed home and froze.

The windows which we had bought from the store when we got the rope stood by the side of the gaping holes.

"I'll surprise Harry", I thought. So with the aid of a keg of six-inch spikes I put them in position and nailed them to the logs — just a temporary measure. I had no fancy window sills — I just blocked up the holes. Driving those spikes into the logs took a lot of energy, but it warmed me up considerably.

By the time Harry returned home for our rabbit stew we were able to look out of the tent flap through glass. He admired my effort but was horrified at the amount of spikes I had used. You can't win all the way! Anyway the windows never blew in.

Next task was the chinking, which posed another problem as the ground was frozen. Here are my three recipes:

No. 1 (if ground not frozen):

    1 large lard pail of water
    1 trowel
    1 hod
    3 parts clay

1 part sand

Method: Cut hay into small pieces to bind. Slap immediately into space between logs.

No. 2 (when ground frozen):

Rear-end material delivered by cow
(preferably hot)

Method: Mix stinking mess with clay from under house, taking care not to undermine foundations. (This proves quite adequate).

No. 3 (desperation):

Chunks of moss from nearest muskeg

Method: Stuff moss into holes as temporary method only. Gales will blow in your face as you sit at meals, and a good-size blizzard will blow the lot out.

I had to settle for No. 2 method, so with hod and trowel I stole into the barn and waited for material to be delivered, then dashed back into the house and whipped up a dollop. Every day I collected my material and worked on the four walls. Even when the chinking was finished it was freezing cold. Our thermometer wasn't much use as it only went down to sixty degrees below zero. Oldtimers said it was at least seventy below and had broken all records. We had no weather reports to confirm the bad news, but *we* knew, it was in our bones!

Another settler went out at this time as he had only frozen hay to feed his stock. He had a nice little team and hayrack which he dumped in our barnyard. Another haircut and he was off.

These horses were smaller than our dear old plugs Skin and Grief. They were named Maud and Mary which embarrassed me as my Christian name was Maud!

I took over Maud and Mary as my team, also the smaller hayrack. Using sleigh runners we were able to speed up the feed problem — two racks at a time every other day.

Wearing snug "long-johns", and Harry's old fur coat which we had rescued from the Vanderveer's, I followed Harry's rack on these hay-lift operations. Each time his rack hit a tree he was at his old lark — axing it down. By the end of the winter he had quite a wide road chopped out.

There were some bad dips on the route — three miles each way. I would close my eyes as his swaying rack whammed into a tree, and offer a prayer that I would get through with my full load and not fall apart. I simply dared not look at Harry's rack ahead which rocked like a ship in a heavy gale.

The howling herd waited impatiently for our return and consumed the hay at a terrific rate. I'll never know why we didn't throw in the sponge — guess we just didn't have one!

During this hard winter another neighbour, an ex-soldier, left a few head of stock in our care. They were a lean, hungry bunch as their owner was unequal to the struggle.

He had a barn of sorts, and as his horses piled up manure behind them he just turned them around. This he did on alternate days but he hadn't allowed for too much of this rotation. The cattle were standing very near the roof when, after struggling with a load of stove pipes, he left a note on his door: "I have given up". So he brought his stock to us and disappeared.

Keeping warm at night was an impossibility. Then Harry had a brainwave — to pull our bed directly under the stove pipes which wound their way from the heater to the cook stove.

The idea was good but alas, to help the fuel problem he had put in some new logs with the dry ones. In the middle of the night I felt rain on my face.

Rousing Harry I said, "It's raining and leaking in on us".

He replied, "Don't be crazy. It never rains when it's as cold as this."

I was not put off so easily and insisted on finding out what was on my face. Harry groped for the matches, lit a candle, looked at me and burst out laughing. I was not so easily amused until I saw his face. We were both spattered by the moisture that comes out of the stove pipes when green wood is burned and mixed with the soot. It was bad enough on our faces which could be washed, but the stains left on our blankets were dyed in for all time.

We had no time for social life at all. But when I heard that there was to be a dance in the schoolhouse I was excited. A notice was posted on the general store announcing the event, and adding, "Bring Your Own Lunch".

Our last social affair had been in the officers' mess at Ripon in Yorkshire. I had enough sense to know it would be nothing like that, but being young I wanted to go. Harry, who was wiser, knew what it would be like and wasn't in the least enthusiastic. I hunted in my trunk for a dress and shoes, and was elated at once again getting into more formal attire.

The schoolhouse was close to our land so we were able to walk there. We left home very late I thought, but I found out that these affairs always started late and went on until milking time the next morning.

Strange sounds were floating from the direction of the schoolhouse. With coyotes howling and dogs barking, I couldn't imagine what it was — but it was music, at least the way it was rendered in these parts.

The sight was an entirely new one for me — oil lamps swinging from the rafters, a scrapy fiddle and an accordion, everyone whirling around in

111

overalls and rubbers, and a huge man shouting. He was calling off a square dance.

I made for a bench at the side of the room and sat down. There was a loud cry. I jumped up and found that I had nearly sat on a baby! I had never thought of taking a baby to a dance. Then looking along the bench I found all the infants of the district rolled up in coats and rugs.

A young lad I knew was sitting at the very end of the bench. I asked him why he wasn't dancing. Sticking out his steaming stockinged feet he replied with a broad grin, "I'm a coolin' off me dogs."

As the sweating dancers warmed up, the smells of the barnyard increased and the music got louder and louder. By the time the ladies talked of lunch we made our excuses to leave.

Tucked up snugly at home in the early hours of the morning, we listened to the melodious jingle of sleigh bells as the merrymakers returned to their remote homesteads. One family had come at least ten miles with their eight children, each of whom had a hot rock at his feet to keep from freezing.

Why does everything have to be done in such a hard way I pondered, as I sank into sleep.

23
Our First Christmas

It was getting near to Christmas and, in a letter from home, mother said she had dispatched our Christmas parcel. Hilda and I arranged to go to St. Lina together to do our shopping and pick up the mail.

Peggy with son Bryan 12 years after leaving the homestead. She is still wearing her warm coyote skin collar, which Harry shot in the bush.

Buster, the Holmes' faithful friend for 17 years, who played an important part in their lives.

Harry and Peggy Holmes at Edmonton's Klondike Days, July 1975. Harry was 87 and Peggy 77.

Below:
Peggy and Harry Holmes at the presentation ceremony by Premier Lougheed of Peggy's homestead painting to the Meadowcroft senior citizens' highrise in Edmonton.

Peggy and her station wagon which she drives every day. December 1979.

Peggy broadcasting one of her homestead scripts on CBC radio in Edmonton.

Writing a radio script on her 65 year old typewriter.

Top:
Cooking for friends. Peggy's parties are famous.

Above:
On her 82nd birthday Peggy entertained some of her neighbours in the Strathcona senior citizens' residence.

The Kilfords had a jumper, which looked like an outdoor toilet on runners, and we decided to take my team, Maud and Mary, for the ten-mile round trip.

It was twenty below zero when we set out, and we intended to keep warm at any cost. It was like preparing for an Arctic expedition, with a charcoal footwarmer, blankets and cushions. At the last minute I threw in my eiderdown quilt. We started out in high spirits, laughing and singing.

With the horses going at a fast clip the whole situation made me giggle. "Wouldn't we make a hit driving along the Strand or King Edward Street?" I said. Then we sang *Let's All Go Down the Strand and Have a Banana*. It's amazing how happy we were with so little, not even a banana!

We did our Christmas shopping at the store and picked up the mail. Yes, the parcel had arrived. We were thrilled, and nothing could destroy our gay mood.

As we passed the Knights' place about half way home, we decided to pay them a visit. We tied up the team to the fence, not bothering to unharness them for such a short stop.

We were given a warm welcome and cups of hot tea. This was a good opportunity to make our Christmas plans. We arranged that the three families, the Holmes, the Knights and the Kilfords, would be together for Christmas dinner at noon at the Knight's home as they were more settled in than we were. We would pool the refreshments. Harry and I would take the roosters, also the cake and pudding which we knew were in the parcel.

Charlie and Etta invited us to stay for supper but we refused as we wanted to get home before dark. We shouted our goodbyes and Merry Christmases, and ploughed through the snow to the team. To our horror, smoke was rising from the jumper in big puffs. We must have kicked over the footwarmer as we got out, and it had been smouldering while we were inside. Thank God there were no flames or we would have had a distracted team and possibly a bad accident. But my longed for Christmas parcel — oh dear, what a mess! It was partially destroyed, and the blankets and quilt were ruined.

We wept all the way home, and were a very different pair from the laughing girls who had set out earlier. We cut off the burned parts of the parcel and managed to retrieve quite a lot. The beautiful rich cake was scorched but the pudding was not too badly burned, and we were thankful to get off so lightly.

Christmas Day was twenty-five below zero with a strong wind. The Kilfords and ourselves went by sleigh in a wagon box, with the sleigh bells ringing and the four of us carrolling all the way to the Knight's.

After a wonderful feast the men relived their old days in the battalion. We girls cleared up and had our own fun, but we had to leave early to attend to the chores. We tried not to think too much of home and to put the memories of past festive seasons out of our minds. Anyway we were all in the same boat — no use feeling sorry for ourselves.

Harry and I invited the others to our home — such as it was at that time — for New Year. So I held my first real dinner party on the homestead, bringing out my Royal Doulton dishes — which actually we used every day as we had no others. Even the chickens pecked out of Royal Doulton!

But with the china shined up, and with gleaming silver, I was proud of my party table. We dressed up in our best clothes, drank moonshine as there were no liquor outlets in those days, and sang in the first day of 1922.

114

Some neighbours dropped in and we received our first introduction to modern music. To me it was ghastly and sounded as if the singers had listened to too many coyotes howling to the moon. But the laugh was on us. One of the young lads went to Edmonton later and became a singing radio personality, teaming up with and eventually marrying Queenie Jackson, a well-known singer.

Well, here was another year to face. We had lined up an ambitious program, the roof to be put on and fencing to be done, together with clearing, breaking, and all the daily chores. Our hearts were strong even if our backs were breaking. But the clarion call of work was ever in our ears.

We rose early as the days never seemed long enough. Every morning at dawn when I pulled my frozen hair off the pillow, I counted my toes. Surprisingly enough they were there — all ten of them. It didn't even help to say "hell", which according to reports would have been hot and most welcome!

At this time the Soldiers' Settlement Board, set up by the Federal Government of Canada, was offering loans at a low rate of interest to soldier farmers.

To carry on with our improvements we had to get some money. We figured that with seven dollars and fifty cents cash per month we could manage to buy our staple foods. Imagine trying to do that today! Butter was then fifteen cents a pound, eggs five cents a dozen, or a bucketful (twenty dozen) for a dollar.

The loan would be used for shingles, seed, grain, wire, etc., so much against our principles we applied for a loan of two hundred and fifty dollars. This we thought was a lot of money to pay back. Some settlers were getting loans of two thousand and three thousand dollars and not worrying at all.

It took us years to pay back our loan. What idiots we were to have been so conscientious, because later the ones who had reneged on their payments came out tops. The government finally cancelled all outstanding debts.

It makes one wonder — could history repeat itself? It has done so. Is credit so easy to get now that the only way to solve the problem would be to cancel all debts again?

Our superhuman effort to keep the stock watered continued. We took from eight in the morning until six at night to get through this mammoth task. The well was just a trickle, so we supplemented our supplies by melting snow on the kitchen stove.

Digging a water hole in a slough on the north boundary of our land was to be the answer. This again proved to be disastrous and, looking back on our life in the bush, I realize tragedy was ever near at hand. We were two against the elements, trying to prove that survival was possible.

After testing and cutting a hole in the ice, Harry figured it would be easier to take the cattle to the water hole instead of hauling the water.

As I watched him on his way to the slough, heading into a bitter north wind, I felt like screaming. But I turned to churning; my butter-making session was a good way to relieve my tension.

When I saw the sorry cavalcade returning, I knew instinctively that something was wrong. After Harry had thawed himself out and was settled before the stove, I asked, "Well, what happened?"

"Things could have been worse," Harry replied. That has been our theme song all our lives and, darn it, he was always right.

Harry told me that the calves had raced ahead, and our dear little calf Toto, grandson of old Croquette the crooked cow with the frozen hooves, was the first at the water hole. He was on his knees having a drink when up slid Grandma, giving him a heavy bump into the hole. Harry had to control the herd and drag Toto out of the water. He kept the calf running all the way home to get his circulation going until he could reach the warmth of the barn. But on arrival, Toto collapsed, frozen to death. Having made pets of our cattle, it was like losing a relative. We couldn't possibly eat Toto; we had raised him.

I was heartbroken as this was our first death on the farm. Our love for each other must have been very strong or we might have considered ending it all. The loaded gun hung on the wall, but it never entered our heads to use it on one another!

As the winter wore on, the cattle were in poorer health, and the sickly ones which we had inherited from neighbours seemed to be on their last legs.

"Look at the gun," Harry said quietly one day. He didn't have to explain as I knew what he had in mind. I shook my head. Yes, it would be merciful to put a few of the worst cases out of their misery. I put my hands over my ears as I heard the shots.

One day Mrs. Keltie dashed in shouting, "Come quickly, Peggy. There's a dead man on the road. He's fallen off his sleigh and I can't move him."

The man was badly frostbitten but not dead — just dead drunk! It was old Tump Evans who had previously lost a leg in another drunken lay-by in the snow.

We dragged him into our kitchen and laid him by the stove. It wasn't long before he came out of his moonshine stupour, sat up and laughed at us!

On one of his later bouts he really did finish himself off. He was either too drunk or too lazy to go outside for firewood, so he hacked a log out of his shack. It wasn't the first time he had used wood in

117

this way and it must have weakened the structure. The shack descended upon him, killing him instantly.

We had some dubious but illustrious neighbours. One of them, Alex Brace, was proud of his direct descent from Jesse James. He tried successfully to live up to the Jesse James image, always toting a gun and shooting on the slightest provocation.

One day he called on me while Harry was in the barn, and waving his six-shooter offered me a dollop of highly potent vanilla extract. I didn't argue but poured some into a glass and pretended to enjoy it. I later hid it in the kitchen cabinet and found it a tasty flavouring for my cakes!

This was the first time I saw Harry really lose his temper. When he came in and saw Brace waving his gun at me, he tossed him out bodily.

Brace prided himself on his veterinary knowledge, telling lurid stories of how he performed internal operations.

Gorily explaining his latest exploit he said, "Well, yer see I take most of the innards out first, then I sees the trouble. Me cow had swallowed a chunk of wire all chewed up into a ball. It was fine 'til I comes to put it back. I'd a chunk of bowel left over so I shoved it back in as best I could."

"Did the cow live?" I asked. Rather a silly question, I admit.

"No," said Brace. "She died a few days later but I sure learned lots from that 'ole cow. Now when it comes to tying up or stitching a cut I 'allus uses the G string off of me violin." Why the G string I never found out.

He kept himself well fortified for his cases and always had a brew coming along. A big X on his calendar marked the day it would be ready. We knew that day without consulting our own calendar, as there was usually a lot of shouting and shooting going on at his place. "Just takin' the cows to water, that's all," he would say. But if a cow got into his garden, bang, as he put it, "beef strewn all over the quarter."

Talking of moonshine, I had an unpleasant experience. One day as Hilda and I were driving home from St. Lina, I was stricken with a blinding headache — unusual for me, but it was a stinker!

As we jogged along the trail we came upon a cheerful looking character swinging a blue enamel tea kettle. We stopped and chatted for a while, but I said I must go as I had a very bad headache.

The man immediately brought out a little tin cup and poured some white liquid from the kettle, which he offered to me saying, "This will cure you." I drank it down, clutched my throat, and thought the top of my head had been blown off.

We said goodbye and hurried home, where I collapsed. Later I found out that he was the district moonshine maker, and this was his most potent brew which he proudly claimed to have matured in the manure pile. That I wouldn't doubt, but it did cure my headache!

Whenever we met up with settlers I always wanted to know how they found this outpost in the first place. No doubt it was my nose for news that gave me this consuming interest.

Harry had already told me about the young honeymooners who had chosen their site by stopping where their old car petered out, and one day I met this former bride. We saw the ancient rusty heap of a car sitting at their sagging gate, so I went in and talked to Mrs. Field. It was difficult to imagine how she looked when she was young, as she was in such a poor condition, physically and mentally. But her children seemed to be strong and husky, and her husband looked virile enough.

I asked her about her births and where she went to have her babies. "I stay right here, and when my time comes I call Bill in from the field and he delivers them," she said stoically.

How she must have suffered! When I see the word pioneer, I never forget the hardships of those first settlers who opened up the country. Here was a happy bride, full of hope but now a human wreck. It looked like the end to me, but it may have been just the beginning as her sons and daughters are probably professionals today. That's the material from which so many of our second and third generations stem.

Bill came in from the barn and told us his story. He said he had been a soldier in the United States Army and had fought in the war between the United States and Spain, following the sinking of the battleship *Maine*. It was a war of very short duration but his government gave him a small pension which was a godsend and made him independent.

Another story remained an unsolved mystery. A homesteader who lost some of his cattle is reported to have gone looking for them, and he disappeared completely. The Mounties searched for him but a fresh fall of snow had covered all tracks. There were no clues and they never found their man. Rumour had it that the man stumbled onto a homesteader's quarter where the slaughtering of cattle was in progress — possibly the cattle he was looking for. No one knew for sure.

Another couple and their small son arrived in the district during the winter on a stoneboat. The horse had a colt which ran behind. Sometimes it tried to get ahead to its mother and would bog down in the deep snow. The long, lanky driver would have to get out, and stomp the snow to get the colt back on the trail.

The parents' seats on the stoneboat were twenty-pound cans of Golden Syrup, and their son sat on fifty pounds of Quaker Oats. It was fairly smooth riding, the woman told me, but freezing cold. The jerking at times would unbalance them and throw them backwards. A balancing act in a circus couldn't have worked harder, she said.

Eventually they had permission to squat in a shack, but the owner soon got tired of his generous offer, and one day when they were away he took out all the windows and buried them in a nearby creek. Her husband found them while out hunting many months later. The wife had come from an estate in England owned by Baron Rothschild. What a shock for her to land up in this wild bush after the manicured gardens and temperate clime of the English village she had left behind.

One of the drawing cards that had lured us to this part of the country was that a railroad had been surveyed, with a town site and "Y" staked a mile or so from our homestead. The grade had been built and everyone lived on hopes. But it was just a political promise that never materialized. It was too far from the little hamlet of Venice to Cold Lake to bring out timber and fish — and hopefully us. The grade was eventually used as a road bed for horse-drawn wagons.

So our dreams never came to pass, but at least we breathed pure air. Although we suffered every inconvenience under the sun, everyone else was in the same boat — and we were happy together.

24
Tea Parties

Spring, heavenly spring at last! We could take our necks out of our coats, straighten up, swing around, open the doors and breathe deeply. I found myself singing, "Spring has come, tra-la-la" all around the barn.

The horses and cattle also responded, and we soon forgot the misery of the winter. The mail lady took the sleigh runners off her ancient auto. That was the only contraption of this sort we had ever seen, and was obviously the forerunner of the snowmobile.

The cattle were now able to drink from the slough. Green grass and pussy willows burst out of the frozen ground. The partridge were drumming, geese honking, ducks quacking, frogs croaking, and the sandhill cranes were flying north. But we had to watch carefully to make sure that the cattle didn't eat the deadly hemlock which grew in profusion around the slough. Remember what hemlock did to Socrates!

It was imperative that we get the roof on our house before the rains came. The second storey logs had to be raised, so Harry and I, with Skin and Grief, once more did the rope trick. After we had rolled the last round into place we celebrated by taking a photo — the end of our only roll of film.

The rafters were not too hard to handle, but the gables were most complicated. We sheeted the roof and then put tar paper on until we could get to the store for shingles when the roads dried.

The Soldiers' Settlement Board loan came through, also one of the inspectors from Edmonton. It was wonderful to have someone from "outside" to visit with. He seemed to be quite worried about us, and seeing our golf clubs stacked in a corner he asked if he could buy them. I don't really think he needed them but felt we could do with some cash. We felt we had made a very profitable deal and the ten dollars was a godsend. We could buy sugar, tea, and flour in large quantities — and stamps for letters home.

There was little travelling while the frost came out of the ground. The trails were a series of mud holes. But when we thought the road was dry enough we decided to go to Ashmont to get shingles, wire, and other necessities. A neighbour's lad came to do the chores while we were away.

So off we went, with Skin and Grief pulling us in the old wagon box. Thirty miles to Ashmont. It took the whole day to get there. The elevator man befriended us and we spent the night at his home. Next day we loaded the shingles, wire, kegs of nails, staples, spikes, also fifty pounds of sugar and one hundred pounds of flour.

The weather was dull and it had rained in the night. We delayed leaving too early, hoping the trail would dry up. As an old native said, "It's a lowery day."

We plodded on from one mud hole to another. The horses were tired and so were we. It was impossible to make it home that night. The only thing to do was to bed down under the stars, so we camped by a slough and threw a tarp on the ground under the wagon box. My pillow was the sugar bag, and Harry's the flour. Wherever we went we took plenty of blankets. Even today I always have one in my car.

I was so exhausted I went to sleep immediately, but suddenly woke up in alarm, banging my head on the wagon box. I thought it was a fire in the bush, but it was the slough — shimmering with myriads of tiny, twinkling lights.

Shaking Harry from his deep sleep I cried, "Look! Fairies with their lanterns." Harry opened one eye slowly, smiled and corrected me. "Glow-worms," he said. It was our own private fantasia.

Needless to say, we were up and on the trail very early. I can't say we were refreshed. Dew on the face is really not so lovely, and it doesn't make for beauty. I felt uncombed, dirty, and weary.

Then back on the trail, with Skin and Grief trustingly plonking along. It was all so peaceful that we gradually forgot our troubles. We thought we were home free when suddenly down they went, up to their bellies in mud. Those poor horses — so helpless, and us so hopeless!

I cried to heaven for help but none came. I suppose they thought up there — you've got yourselves into this mess, now get yourselves out!

Harry dug out each hoof — all eight of them. I held the reins and took orders. This was indeed a calamity. As I yelped and helped — Buster barking frantically — I declared emphatically, "I shall never *ever* laugh again!"

The team went down twice before we succeeded in getting them out. A third time and we'd have had to call it a dead loss. It took us a long while to get going again, and we looked a sad, bedraggled pair.

After another hour on the trail something amused me, and I found myself laughing heartily.

"I thought you were never *ever* going to laugh again," said Harry. "You should never make definite statements if you can't live up to them."

Once back home we had to start tackling our house-building operation, and to figure out how to design our high-pitched roof. Our scaffolding was somewhat unsteady and it was a tricky task. I started as a jo-boy but soon became a shingler. The highs and lows in this life were terrific!

While we were busy on the roof, a neighbour, Albert Brook, came out of the bush after hibernation. Formerly of the Household Guards, he was over six feet tall and very elegant, the sort of Englishman the down-to-earth Canadian homesteader cannot tolerate. He'd come to borrow a nail file of all things — not a pitchfork or a rake, but a nail file!

Brook looked disapprovingly at what we were doing, but he delighted me when he said, "Really Mrs. Holmes, fancy you going up on the roof. I will come over tomorrow and help Mr. Holmes to shingle."

Tomorrow came, but no Brook. At noon he ambled in, just in time for lunch. After a good meal he offered to do the dishes.

"But aren't you going on the roof to shingle?" I asked.

"No, Mrs. Holmes. I have a phobia and can't stand heights. Possibly I could chop some wood."

He tested the axe and said it wasn't sharp enough, so with that he disappeared into the bush until the next noon when he smelt our rabbit stew.

So Harry and I shingled vigorously with no help. We were no "fiddlers on the roof" but we really worked fast. There was only an odd bit to finish so we decided to call it a day. I set a nice supper table and this was to be a feast.

Our chores were done and we sat down with a glow of satisfaction at our great accomplishment.

Suddenly, crackle, crackle, crackle!

"My God, the roof's on fire," Harry shouted.

Up the scaffold he scrambled with a bucket of water. Our fire department of two had to douse the flames. We found that the stove pipe had come out of the stove jack. My beautiful supper table was washed out but the damage to the roof was fortunately not too bad. Our quick thinking and action had saved our home.

With a roof over our heads our home was beginning to look very cosy with cretonne curtains and cushions, a Wilton rug, a Morris chair, draped orange boxes nailed together for a vanity dresser, bedside tables, etc. Thank heavens for wooden orange boxes — double deckers with a shelf provided. Large round wooden cheese boxes covered to match the curtains added to the Canadiana look, often strived for today. Harry had made some bookshelves which ran across one end of the room. Plato and his pals looked rather out of place, but they consoled us during the long winter nights. The staircase to the second storey was rough and rather unsafe, having no bannisters, but was much stronger than the ladder usually used by the homesteaders.

With all this "luxury" I decided it was time to give a tea party, so I invited a neighbour, Mrs. Sanford, Hilda Kilford and Etta Knight. I prepared some dainty dishes including cream tarts, a concoction I'd last tasted in a select tea room in England.

Mrs. Sanford was from the backwoods of Virginia. She had a fascinating habit of clutching her breast, rolling her eyes heavenward, and exclaiming, "Shoot, I said to Daddy!" Why he never did when he had so many tempting offers I failed to understand.

All was going very happily until Mrs. Sanford suddenly put her hand over her mouth and choked. We tried not to notice, but when she stood up, struck her dramatic pose saying, "Shoot — I'm off!" we were left wondering, could it have been my cream tarts?

Later I asked her. "Shoot!" she replied. "I jest

broke me tooth on yer tart." Nothing seemed to go right. Were we jinxed?

However, Mrs. Sanford didn't seem too perturbed and returned my tea invitation shortly after. Hilda and I were the only guests.

Harry got the horses and wagon ready for us, and away we went to our first real tea party in the north.

The Sanfords' home was a fairly large one-room log shack which apparently housed eight. As we entered this dark, overheated cavern we felt like pit ponies. Groping our way to two chairs we looked around. There was a large double bed at one end of the room with a picture of Abraham Lincoln frowning down disapprovingly. The two pillows stood erect as sentinels, both decorously covered with large red pocket handkerchiefs.

The heater, like something out of a battleship, was operating like a blast furnace at peak production time. This our hostess stoked with long logs which she pushed in every time she passed by.

On the huge kitchen range a black skillet full of water simmered away with globules of grease floating on top. To my dismay, Mrs. Sanford threw this greasy water into a large enamel coffee pot. My stomach turned over as I realized this was the tea. By this time I daren't look at Hilda. I was a giggler, and I knew if once touched off we were done for.

"Put your legs under the table," said Mrs. Sanford. The table — heaven help us — appeared to be set for a multitude of threshers or a good-sized wake. Moose meat, sauerkraut, pickles, potato salad, hunks of bread, pies, and — to return the compliment — cream tarts.

Hilda and I took one look and gasped. Buster sat at my feet under the table. The dreadful part of this was that Mrs. Sanford refused to sit down. She waited on us like honoured guests at a Hilton Hotel.

Every time she left us to stoke the heater I shoved hunks of moose meat into Buster's mouth. The darned dog chewed with no manners at all, and we had to talk in loud voices to cover up the fact that we were getting rid of it under the table.

When the orgy was over we staggered to our wagon, Mrs. Sanford shouting, "Shoot! It's sure bin nice having youse folks."

We drove out of sight — we hoped! Then Hilda jumped down from her side of the wagon and I from mine, and we both vomited. Buster, too, was upset. It was no use, we just couldn't take it. "Shoot no!"

25
The Fire Ranger

Clearing! That must be done, and the quickest way possible was by fire. Bonfires were fun and games, but the idea of an honest-to-goodness bush fire, even while the ground was still fairly wet, appalled me.

"Don't put us through that peril," I pleaded.

Harry pointed out with glee that a good old blaze would do more work in a short time than he could in twenty years.

"Our precious home! How can we protect it?" I asked.

"With a fireguard," he replied. "A trench around our property."

Skin and Grief took a dim view of ploughing around the buildings to provide this guard, and I took care to busy myself with household chores while my arsonist husband was burning up the countryside.

Smoke was belching high into the sky from the nearby bush. The method Harry used was crude but effective. Riding his saddle horse, he threw lighted matches behind them. They were matches with a delayed action. My God, when I think of it now! Dangerous — I'll say it was.

While I was praying and working, trying not to think of destruction and utter ruin, I heard a loud authoritative rap on the door. On opening it I saw a short stocky man, very important-looking with his coat open, and a flashing badge on his shirt — just like a sheriff in the movies.

Glaring at me, he announced, "Oim the foir ranger oi am. 'Oo set that there foir?" You didn't have to be a Professor Higgins to know he was a cockney.

"Where's yer 'usband?" he asked.

I dilly-dallied while the smoke was nearly choking us. Then drawing myself up with as much dignity as possible I replied, "Mr. Holmes is away."

"Looks ta me 'e's making 'ell out in yon bush. Some blaze 'e's got there!" Screwing up his face and apparently deep in thought he added, "'Olmes did yer say? Not 'Arry 'Olmes hof the 31st Battalion?"

"Yes."

"Ow, that's different. Yer see hoi was 'is sergeant-major and a farver to them boys."

Smiling at each other and the official badge no longer flashing so brightly, I invited him in and we chatted while the fire raged. His 'Arry could have set the world on fire.

We discussed many things; he appeared to be an

expert on every subject.

"Ow do yer feed yer 'ens?" he asked.

"We give them grain," I replied.

"Do yer use an 'opper?"

"An 'opper, what's that?" I asked. "No, we just use Royal Doulton, that's all we have."

"Well, yer needs an 'opper." And he proceeded to give me a lesson on hopper feeding.

We continued our animated conversation over endless cups of tea until at last Harry returned, looking like a smoked haddock.

The ex-Sergeant-Major threw himself at "'is buddie".

"'Arry 'ow are yer, me boy?" he boomed. "Remember Sergeant-Major Thompson?"

Harry did indeed. The remainder of the evening was spent in recounting war-time anecdotes. Fire was never mentioned except the fire on the western front.

After serving him a good meal we thought he'd be off. No sir! He was "in no 'urry."

He had arrived on horseback with a foal running with its mother. Feed was none too plentiful after the hard winter, but that did not concern this official. He decided to spend the night. Fair enough — but a week later we were ready to throw him out.

One choice piece of wisdom that dropped from his lips he gave to us freely: "Oi never woiks, oi negowshiate!"

Then he presented us with an expense sheet, a blank one, which naturally had to be signed. Just another rip-off — his own little Watergate! Laughing heartily as he rode away we decided how right he was. Why "woik" when you can "negowshiate"?

26
Lady with a Lamp

Now that we had a few acres cleared and ploughed, our next job was seeding. We decided to put in wheat, so Harry went forth to sow.

With a large basket under his arm and a strap around his neck he scattered the seed rhythmically over the earth. To see this lonely figure walking into one of our spectacular sunsets was a spiritual experience — so very biblical. In fact Harry looked like Jesus, although come to think of it I don't remember seeing a picture of Jesus actually sowing seed. He walked through the fields rubbing the grain in his hands. Hopefully the crop would come later!

Meanwhile a fence had to be put around the crop otherwise our ever-hungry herd would soon have polished it off. We were lucky to get some spools of barbed wire at St. Lina, so we worked quickly and endlessly. After a particularly long hard day there was just one more strand to do. It was late and we were tired and ravenous. Just one more pull was needed on the stretchers when, horrors, something slipped and the barbed wire dragged through Harry's hand. It caught me on the wrist, but my gash was nothing compared to my husband's torn bleeding palms.

How terribly tired and sorry for ourselves we felt, but the situation had to be faced. Torn hands had to be fixed up — no time for self pity in our schedule.

There were plenty of emergencies to be dealt with, and neighbours constantly called on us for help.

One day Mrs. Sanford came dashing in, "Shoot! Where's yer man?"

"He's away fencing. What's the trouble?"

"It's one of our cows," she replied. "She's dying in yon pasture."

Not being a vet, but willing to try anything, I offered my services. Away we went. It was a pitiful sight to see this poor animal lying on her back with her legs uphill, threshing around and moaning in abject misery. She certainly was in bad shape. All I could think of was, if she's going to die we'd better make her comfortable. I knew I would hate to die with my legs uphill!

"Quick, let's turn her over," I said. So grabbing her legs we managed to heave this tortured creature over — a very dangerous act as she could have kicked us in the teeth.

But we apparently performed a miracle. Rosie rolled her eyes in grateful thanks, got to her feet leisurely, walked away and started to munch the grass.

There were many experts in the district, and when we told them about this life-saving act they remarked casually, "Oh, she was just bloated." It just shows what gas will do for you if you happen to be lying uphill!

Another calamity occurred when one of the settlers who had come in at the same time as us was alone on his homestead. His wife was in hospital in the city and he had cut his knee very badly with his axe. We fixed him up, but he had to lay up for some weeks, so he and his stock were brought over to us. There was nothing else I could do. Mr. Steinbeck was a member of the Plymouth Brethren and gave us a big dose of religion. His philosphy was simple; you were saved if you just crossed an imaginary line. From them then on you didn't have to worry; everything was taken care of. It didn't do me any good, but it was apparently a comfort to him.

The next call for help came from one of the war brides who had come over from England in the same ship as we did. Her young son dashed into our yard crying, "Can you come at once? Mum needs you!"

As I quickly saddled Mignon and cantered off I wondered what the next episode would be in this ever unfolding soap opera.

I found Flo lying on her bed. She was pregnant and in extreme pain. She had been alone for some time as her husband was away in the bush.

She was obviously very sick and needed expert medical help, which was a tall order in these parts. The nearest doctor lived at St. Paul, thirty miles away, and his fee of a dollar a mile and ten dollars a visit was far out of the reach of most of the settlers.

Then I remembered hearing of an old man known as "Doc" who lived about six miles north at Beaver River Crossing. The title didn't really mean a thing in this country — even a bootlegger was called "Doc".

No one knew much about him but he was my only hope. So I rode off to find this mysterious doctor, eventually arriving at a well-kept little home where an old lady came out to greet me. I told her my story and pleaded for her husband to come to our aid.

"Homer hasn't a licence to practise in Canada", she said. "We came up from the States and he has retired."

However I persuaded her to rouse the doctor from his afternoon nap, and after much coaxing, and a stiff tot of moonshine administered by his wife, he consented to come with me.

"Doc" was a real show-off! After we had saddled

his horse he took a flying leap onto its back, missed it and landed on his own back on the other side! We picked him up and heaved him onto the saddle. It wasn't a very auspicious start!

We must have looked an odd couple — this old man and young girl cantering along the trail. As we neared our journey's end I turned to speak to him but, to my horror, he was belting for home as fast as his horse could carry him.

My heart sank to think I had him so near to our destination and then had to lose him. This I couldn't allow to happen without an explanation. So I turned Mignon round and raced after him, shouting, "Hi Doc, come back! Where do you think you're going?"

By the time I caught up to him the old doc was breathless but I managed to hear, "My bag, I've forgotten my bag." His little black bag which had not been used for years. He had come without it.

I could see it was no use arguing so I returned to my sick friend and explained that the doctor was on his way. True to his word he eventually arrived, nearly done for I'll admit, but complete with his precious bag.

He diagnosed the case — undulent fever — and said she must get to a hospital or she would die. He gave her some pain killer, and then was off. We were grateful for his advice and I hope the College of Physicians and Surgeons never caught up with him for practising without a licence!

Hilda and I cared for Flo until she was able to travel, and her child had a better fate than her last baby son who had died in the shack when only a few weeks old, and whom she had helped to bury.

Heartbreaks are left in many places — little graves, lonely and forsaken. I thought of my baby daughter who I had left behind in a lonely plot in Edmonton.

The Dunstall family left the district after this — another unequal struggle against the elements.

Amazingly enough, I met Flo fifty years later in a nursing home in White Rock, B.C. We relived those days and cried together over some of our experiences. She told me the baby lived and was able to walk before she did! Old Doc had been right in his diagnosis.

27
Mail Order Bride

Every day I would take a look at our crop. It fairly jumped out of the earth and looked green and healthy. Everything seemed to be running smoothly. The big jobs were gradually ticked off our staggeringly long list.

One sunny afternoon we had to pick up some supplies from our local store a few miles away, so Harry hitched up the wagon and I climbed up beside him. Skin and Grief plodded along the track and all was peaceful. It was a glorious day — the sort they sang about later in *Oklahoma!* — *Oh What a Beautiful Mornin', Oh what a Beautiful Day*. In my hazy dream world at that time I was thinking of *Come to Kew in Lilac Time*.

It's strange what this life does to one. Suddenly, for no apparent reason, I let out a bloodcurdling scream. The horses were terrified and bolted as fast as they could go. Using all his strength, Harry tried to pull them up, but no way would they stop. They were going hell bent for leather after such an experience.

The wagon box was somewhat rickety and I was rocked out of my screaming jag. But I really did feel much better. Finally Harry won the day and Skin and Grief slowed up, panting and foaming.

"For God's sake, whatever was the matter?" Harry asked.

"Nothing, nothing at all," I replied. "I just felt the urge to scream."

"Well, if you ever get that urge again, go behind the barn and do it — and let me know beforehand or you'll scare the livestock to death."

I did this many times and, believe me, it relieves tension. I am sure Freud would have suggested other therapeutic methods, but I can assure you that a jolly good scream behind the barn really helped! I had to curb myself later when we lived in the city. Even one scream in the garage behind closed doors would probably have been followed by police sirens and a visit from the arms of the law.

Spring was an exciting season despite the arrival of the huge bloodsucking mosquitoes, "no-see-ems" (gnats), and "bulldogs" (big black flies). The bots which swelled up under the hides of the cows were also bad. I became an expert at de-botting. Should you care to take up this hobby, you use your two thumbs, use pressure, and if you are lucky out pops the bot. Revolting but necessary!

Buster had no fear of coyotes and often had a tussle with them. One day he tackled two coyotes in the bush. On this occasion he was obviously getting the worst of the fight so Harry took aim with his .22 rifle. It was a lucky shot; he hit one coyote and the other ran away. But Buster was saved.

Harry's bag was a prize skin which we tanned and made into a warm collar for me for our next severe winter.

Mrs. Plymouth, our pet hen, also got into a fight with a chicken hawk. She lost her tail feathers but valiantly saved her brood. It was the survival of the fittest and we were all in there pitching. Mrs. Plymouth had to protect her chicks every year and proudly brought them all in from the bush. However hungry we were, we could never have eaten Mrs. Plymouth. She laid the tastiest eggs, and it broke my heart when I had to part with her when we left the bush for the city lights.

Spring was an unsettling time for several of us, including one neighbour, Herman Brueker, a lonely widower whose wife had died in childbirth leaving him with four young children. So came our next challenge — an unusual one. Herman asked us to advertise for a wife for him. This was something new for me; I knew one could buy practically anything — if one had the cash — from Eaton's catalogue, but ordering a wife was an entirely different kettle of fish!

Herman arrived at our place brandishing a newspaper *The Winnipeg Free Press and Prairie Farmer* which ran a matrimonial column for lonely hearts.

"I want you folks to help me get a new missus," he announced. "It ain't no use; I can't do everything on me own, what with the kids and the chores, and feeding the stock. I've got to get me a woman but I ain't no good at this writin' stuff."

This was a diversion for me and sounded like fun. Harry and I both realized that Herman would need help to compose his letters if he were to get this matrimonial deal under way. Ads were cheap in those days, and I remember they were very long and detailed.

We read through the Lonely Hearts columns

with Herman, burning our coal oil lamp well into the night. The advertisements extolled the virtues of girls and women who were offering themselves as companions, housekeepers — or preferably brides.

Although it was amusing it had its tragic side. When I read what they had to offer a picture flashed before me of the slave days when black women and children were sold off by auctioneers. Although we had advanced since then, here surely was another form of slavery in the northern bush.

Herman, Harry and I went through the list of virgins carefully but we were not impressed. We all made different choices but, of course, the final decision had to rest with Herman. Dash it all, she was going to be his life partner — we hoped!

We drafted a letter to the *Free Press and Prairie Farmer*, enclosing the requested dollar and giving him a terrific buildup.

"Herman Brueker is a solid settler from eastern Canada with a German background," I wrote. "A Protestant, absolutely no vices, brown eyes, light coloured hair, and a good worker."

I hoped this didn't sound too much like one of the dreadful slave bills of the olden days. I also enclosed a faded snapshot taken in his youth. I'm afraid it didn't resemble him much at this time of courtship. I had thought of enclosing one of Jack Buchanan, the matinée idol of my day, but that would have been too unfair!

After this emotional decision Herman brought out a bottle of his home brew which we declined. It was too powerful for us; besides we hoped to keep our eyesight intact.

As payment for our help he even offered us a cow. "No thank you," I declared emphatically. That would have meant another mouth for us to feed. We already had enough scrubs running around consuming our precious hay.

"God, am I ever glad you folks helped me out," said Herman. "I'm a no-gooder when it comes to this courtin' stuff."

It took about a month to get the first reply. Several came in but were unsuitable, mostly widows with large hordes of children which was the last thing Herman wanted. It would have been worse than trying to bring up his four alone. At last he drove up to the house waving a letter and grinning from ear to ear.

"Hi folks, look at this 'ere letter from a Nellie Waters. She's sent a snap and all. Ain't she sumpin'? Couldn't have done better on a dark night if I'd had me lantern lit."

The letter listed Nellie's many virtues and apparently no vices. I'm afraid Harry and I were a bit sceptical. The letter could have been written by someone else. Wasn't that what we were doing? And the snap could have been taken years ago.

Herman answered at once — at least I answered and Harry wrote the letter as we thought it should be in a man's handwriting. Nellie replied on the dot, and an enquiry elicited the information that she was a widow with one young son, and that her late husband had gone out in a boat on Lake Ontario and had never returned. Harry and I were still a little worried. Was the story true? Also the name Mrs. Waters sounded phoney, especially when tied into the lake episode. But Herman seemed satisfied.

We continued to read Nellie's letters and to compose replies. We did not mislead her as to the hardships of life in the bush, and told her about Herman's four young children; so she knew the score. Things must have been desperate for her in eastern Canada to consider such a drastic step, but she appeared to be willing to risk it.

Herman decided to send for his bride-to-be well before the harvesting season. So he forwarded the money for her fare and planned to pick her up at the station at Ashmont, the end of the rail line.

At the last moment he began to cuss about "having to import" a woman. "It's too damned expensive and then a guy never knows what kind of ornery filly she's likely to turn out," he complained. It never occurred to him that the girl might be getting the worst of the bargain.

The day of her arrival dawned, and Herman, after much spit and polish, left to meet her. We thought they would get married at Ashmont but although she apparently came up to expectations Herman decided they would live "on approval", which they did for six months.

This was quite a shock to me as marriage was still an institution as far as I was concerned, but the romance prospered and Herman was so pleased with his bargain that he offered a cow to a young bachelor living nearby if he would do the same thing — just to settle up the country.

The young man pondered the suggestion for a time, but rejected it, declaring "I'm no pioneer."

Herman brought Nellie over to see us soon after her arrival. They were accompanied by their whole brood of five. Nellie was thin and rather sad looking. Life had certainly not been good to her and, as I thought, the snap she had sent had been taken many years previously. But the children all seemed happy with their new "Mum" and she had agreed to shack up with Herman to see how things worked out.

A few months later Nellie, looking worn and tired, called in to see me. She told me she was pregnant, but Herman had promised that as soon as he had time he would take her to town to get married. "He's good to me and I like his kids," she said.

It was well after Christmas before Herman took Nellie to their wedding in town, with sleigh bells ringing. She was to remain at Ashmont until after the birth of her baby. Herman was taking no chances with his mail-order bride after the dramatic experience of his first wife's delivery.

I was waiting in their shack with the children when the newlyweds returned with their baby. The Brueker children were excited and crowded around their new little sister. Nellie proudly showed me her shining new gold wedding ring.

So we were responsible for what turned out to be a happy marriage, thanks to the *Free Press and Prairie Farmer* and the fates that decreed this meeting. Such was the spirit of the true pioneer. Brigham Young had several wives to fall back on, but these homesteaders had to make do with one, even if it meant ordering sight unseen!

28
Bath Night in the Bush

Saturday — far from being a rest day after the week's labours — was a heavy one for me, as that was the day reserved for my laundry and our weekly baths.

Flossie, as we christened our old cook stove, was packed with logs and belched like someone with an overloaded stomach.

Harry got down the large tin tub from its nail on the back wall of the house, and we started a bucket parade from the well. In the winter we just scooped up the deep snow.

Flossie devoured logs at a terrific rate, so I had to use all this extra heat to boil our clothes in an old copper boiler, and warm the two "sad irons" for the ironing.

How I longed for good old Lottie, our washerwoman at home. She would have been horrified to see me at work with our rickety hand-operated washing machine which we had acquired in one of our swap deals. Money seldom changed hands between the homesteaders as we were all broke.

Turning the handle to swish the clothes around was a heavy job, and Harry often came in to help me before I collapsed with exhaustion.

Our heavy underwear, thick sweaters, and Harry's work overalls and woollen socks were difficult to get clean with our primitive apparatus. I always had several long skirts and petticoats to wash as there were no jeans in those days, although I wore breeches for riding.

We had no drip and dry; it was more like drip and freeze. I've taken many weird shapes off the clothes line, and tried my darndest to get them through the door. Talk about the abominable snowman! I'd hate to do *his* laundry!

In the summertime we would take turns with the handle, and one of us would watch the smudge — our fire screen — to try to keep the mosquitoes off. Mosquito bites were far worse than the chilblains I suffered in England during my schooldays.

In fact, I was inspired to verse by those pesky mosquitoes which would not leave me alone. One of my efforts, which I called *The Ubiquitous Mos-*

quito, was pinned onto the door of our house. I still remember a bit of it:

> *Delicious blood,*
> *How easy,*
> *How sweet,*
> *How sweaty.*

There was usually some crisis in the middle of wash day. A cow would calve, a horse would cut himself on the barbed wire fence, or the cattle would get loose. I generally ended up by finishing the job alone.

Believe me, I cut down on the ironing. The very name "sad iron" lowered my spirits. But, silly me, I still used a white tablecloth for our meals, which gave me "royal" status in the district. I guess the neighbours thought I was stuck-up, but I maintained the family tradition for my own sake.

The saying that the family that prays together stays together could be changed to the family that washes together stays together. On wash day with the two of us, Buster, and Mrs. Plymouth, our pet hen pecking and clucking nearby, any passerby — if there had been one — would have thought we were running a three-ring circus.

On Saturday night, after I had finished the laundry, Harry would come in, tired out, to help me fill the tin tub with water from the copper boiler. While it was heating we would listen to our tinkly gramophone blasting out the *Anvil Chorus*. I dared not let myself think about the well-appointed bathroom I'd left over six thousand miles away.

I was first in the tub. The water was hard, alkaline and scummy. I had to wash my hair at the same time and, as I wore it long, as was the custom, it took quite a while to dry. Luckily I had enough natural curl to allow me to pin it up into some kind of style.

Of course I had no face creams or makeup, but I usually wore a big sunhat so my complexion wasn't too weatherbeaten.

We hadn't heard about Yoga but we quickly adopted the Buddha position in order to fit into the round tub. With a bar of Lifebuoy soap I tried in vain to whip up a lather. Needless to say, I didn't linger over my ablutions.

Once I was out of the tub Harry climbed in. As I looked at the hollow bomb hole in his backside, I was grateful that, after the horror of the war, we were able to be together. And as I scrubbed his back everything seemed to be right with the world.

Buster frisked around and could hardly wait for Harry to get out of the tub when he plunged in, wagging his tail furiously.

We usually locked the door before starting to bathe, but one night we forgot and, while Harry was in the tub, a long nose and two beady eyes peered around the door.

I rushed to the door to discover an ancient, delapidated-looking man and a young boy outside with a skinny horse and rickety wagon. The man had come to sell us some patent medicine — a cure-all for humans and animals alike. I don't know whether you were supposed to drink it or rub it on but I hadn't the heart to turn away this odd couple at such a late hour. We never took medicine, and hadn't even provided ourselves with a box of aspirins to take into the bush. The only remedy we had was Nux Vomica for the horses.

The bottle was only twenty-five cents, but any wandering traveller always expected to be put up for a day or two — sometimes a week — with free board and feed for his horse. So by the time we were through, that twenty-five cent bottle had cost us plenty.

This old hobo was full of tall stories, some of which were quite amusing. He called himself doctor, and sometimes professor, but we knew nothing about him except what his grandson Dwight told us. According to him, "grandpappy", who came from the States, had shot one of his neighbours and had been charged with murder. He had managed to escape over the border with his grandson, and had taken to the road. Ten-year-old Dwight was really proud of "grandpappy", and embellished his tall stories with further gory details which we could hardly believe.

Dwight was a cute kid, but oh so dirty! I wanted to dunk him in the bathtub which was still full when he arrived, but Buster had jumped in after Harry and so the opportunity was lost.

Anyway we bedded the two of them down in the barn for a couple of nights, and when they left my heart went with them. What would become of them, and how would Dwight get any education?

It was on Saturday after washday and bathnight — when Flossie was at her hottest — that I would put a few tins of dough in the oven. Oh how good that smell was of newly-baked bread, which I would cut in thick slices and serve with homemade baked beans as a Sunday treat.

I was always trying to invent some way to make life easier, and the log pile was a losing battle. To keep up the supply took hours of valuable work time. I know the sound of a saw is considered musical, but it grated on my ears, and I was infuriated that all that beautiful timber — not to mention muscle power — was just going up in smoke.

One day the smell of the Red Top hay which I was hauling for the cattle brought back a memory. I remembered the haybox cooking we had done during World War I in England.

The government had asked everyone to conserve

energy, and one of the ways to do this was haybox cooking. I tried to recall how it was done. The first thing was to get a tea chest. Would the store in St. Lina have one? They had always been able to provide me with orange boxes for my homemade furniture, but I wondered if they would carry anything so dignified as a tea chest. However, my brainwave worked. Majeau, the owner of the store, did have a tea chest which he insisted on giving to me, so I was in business.

First I filled it with hay. God knows I was always sitting on a load of the stuff; no difficulty there. But it had to be layered with newspapers. We never had papers except *John Bull, Tidbits*, and the odd overseas *Mirror* my parents sent from England, so I had to scrounge around.

First I put a stewpot on the stove to boil — always the inevitable rabbit. Then I put it in the hay box before we sallied forth for our day's work. We came home to a perfectly cooked dinner, and the log pile was not lowered at all.

So my tea chest had a place of honour beside the old cook stove, and we really saved wood. I guess this hay box was the forerunner of today's crockpot.

29
Rabbits and Raspberries

The seasons seemed to follow each other more and more quickly. From a short spring to summer with another dramatic change of climate. But our health was robust, and I realize now that we lived like the health nuts of today.

The early pigweed or lamb's quarter made a tasty green vegetable; dandelion leaves were excellent for salad. Then there was wild mint with which I made peppermint tea, also blueberries, high and low bush cranberries, raspberries and wild strawberries. The garden and crop seemed to spring miraculously out of the ground. It was a veritable Garden of Eden with no apples but an abundance of mosquitoes.

Busy as I was, I always looked forward to news from home. Letters came telling me about weekends on Harry's houseboat, the *Ariadne*, yachting parties on the River Humber, and family gatherings. It was all meant to cheer me up, but my family's well-meaning efforts often plunged me into the depth of despair and homesickness. Homesickness is worse than seasickness. I've had them both! Seasickness stops when you step off the boat; I could hardly step off the land.

This was particularly hard on Harry. He tried to cheer me up in many ways. But I hit a low that summer; I even got past the screaming behind the barn point. I would saddle Mignon and urge her into her fastest gallop. Riding was not as exciting in the bush country as it had been dashing over the uncluttered ranges east of Calgary, but it was one way to blow my low spirits to the four winds, and I would return telling myself how lucky I was to have my own horse — and who wanted to go boating anyway?

One day a lonely bachelor, Ed Nelson, came to offer us help on the homestead if he could stay with us for a day or so. We were delighted as an extra pair of hands was always welcome. But on the first day in the bush he managed to miss the tree he was chopping and buried the axe in his knee. This necessitated a trip to the doctor, who was thirty miles away, as it was an ugly gash and had to be stitched.

So our visitor lingered for what seemed a long while — a cot case added to our already overflowing schedule. Fate seemed to decree that we had to do all our work alone.

Soon after this came the news that a neighbour had lost a baby boy. She was all alone as her husband had gone out to make a stake.

Feeling very concerned, I went over to offer sympathy and help. It was a poor one-room log shack, a temporary shelter until her husband could build a home. This frail, dignified lady, Mrs. Crandall, was ill-equipped to face this rugged pioneer life.

As I knocked on her door she said, "Do come in and sit down." She didn't come to the door so I let myself in.

Mrs. Crandall was facing a small makeshift dresser and looking into a mirror. She finished brushing and pinning up her hair as if there were an invisible wall between us. In her imagination she was alone in her dressing room! Then, turning around, she gave me a reception such as I might have expected in a baronial mansion.

We talked together quietly for a time; my hostess sat facing the window and I had my back to it. Later she went into her imaginary kitchen to make tea. All she really did was to turn to the cook stove.

All this time my mind was working at full speed. Where is the dead baby? No sign of it. I tried to look under the bed without getting up. No box — nothing. My nerves were taut and I realized that we were whispering. I wonder why one feels compelled to whisper when facing death in any form. Silly really, because a corpse can't hear — or can it? I had some strange experiences in later years.

Mrs. Crandall turned to me with a very sweet expression and asked, "Would you like to see the little man?"

"Yes," I replied timidly.

"Well, you'll have to move. You are resting on the coffin."

I sprang up and turned around. Sure enough, a small rough box lay on the window sill among the plants which had been pushed aside. No wonder I hadn't seen it; it had been behind me all the time.

He was a dear little baby. His mother's pathetic attempts to trim the interior with soft white linen and bits of lace made me cry. I left her so alone but calmly resigned.

A few weeks later she came over to visit me. "That's a nasty tear you have in your skirt," I remarked. "Yes," she replied, "I must mend it. I tore it when we buried the baby."

Her husband was still away so some neighbours had taken her to the nearest graveyard a few miles away. As the sky became stormy they had to make a fast move for home and she had helped to fill in the grave, tearing her skirt on the handle of the shovel.

These tragedies took a toll on me. I was over sensitive; maybe I was getting "shock treatments" early in life.

On the day I returned home from Mrs. Crandall's I was in a sober frame of mind, but determined not to let things get me down. Harry was out in the bush so I decided to help him by starting the chores and to stop dwelling on the calamities which seemed to surround us.

However this was a bad idea as in the crowded barn one of the horses accidentally trod on my foot. Grief was no thoroughbred but she had the feet of a Clydesdale! It was an earthen floor with a layer of hay, otherwise I might have had a permanent injury.

I screamed in Grief's ear, startling her to such an

extent that she reared up on her hindlegs while I dashed out of the barn screaming to the heavens. No doubt I scared a few coyotes in addition to our livestock. But the heavens revolved in their orderly pattern and paid no attention to my yelling.

I returned to the house, limping and subdued. I must go back to England, I thought. This isolation is too much for me. I tugged at my hair and was ready to scream again but managed to control myself. The tiny shack seemed to close in on me. However did I get into this wilderness? It was love, of course. But how long would this young love last?

The smell of the rabbit stew even though tastily spiced, was nauseating to me, and the darned cows were at the door, mooing to be milked.

Damn the cows. Let their udders burst. I'd had it. Where was this man I'd crossed the Atlantic with? Chopping trees, mending fences, mucking out the barn. There were thousands of jobs to be done besides the everyday chores. The loneliness was unbearable.

I had had another letter from home which had triggered this foul mood. This time the news was about the latest play at the theatre. I was hundreds of miles from one. Then I remembered our happy picnics on the beach. I was at least a thousand miles from the sea.

My cousins told me about the arrival of another new baby. Well, I mused, I have a new colt and a calf. I also read about the latest fashions. I looked at my outfit, a secondhand bus conductor's uniform, blue with silver buttons, even a coat-of-arms on the pocket. It wasn't bad for this primitive neck of the woods, but I had to admit that it was not the latest style.

When Harry returned, oozing fresh air and the joy of living, I was ready for him.

"How much cash have you?" I demanded. Harry looked startled.

"I'm leaving," I explained. "I simply can't stand this life any longer. A hundred and sixty acres of rabbits and trees; that's all it is, even when you have proved it up. What have you got? Rabbits and trees — and, oh yes, a smoking muskeg!"

My patient husband stood there smiling at my tantrum. But this was no childish outburst. It was a woman ready to go anywhere to get away from the howling coyotes, the ever-hungry herd, the endless chores, the suffocating forest, and the sameness of everything.

"Well my dear," he replied. "How much cash have I got? Let me look."

After foraging around for a few minutes he returned to announce, "It's exactly seven dollars and fifty cents."

That settled it. I was stuck. If it had been ten dollars I could have escaped. It would have been just enough to get me by train to Edmonton or Calgary if I had hitch-hiked the first thirty miles.

Harry went out quietly and closed the door of the shack behind him. I sobbed uncontrollably, feeling totally abandoned.

About fifteen minutes later he returned with a large leaf full of the most delicious raspberries. Our surprising wilderness had yielded this luscious dish. I threw out the rabbit stew and we feasted on raspberries and fresh cream from our herd.

My black mood disappeared. Let them have their theatres, fine clothes, and babies. I had my man who could produce the most delightful, magical surprises at the right moment. That was what our love was about.

30
The Bear Scare

Fall with its flambuoyant colours and woodsy tang in the air gave us a happy respite before our second winter clamped down and plunged us once more into the deep freeze.

A few new settlers had come into the district between our home and hay quarters. One day an attractive red-headed girl came through our yard on her way to get the mail at a mail stop about a couple of miles away. She was carrying a rifle. She told me her name was Bernice Elder and that she'd been a secretary in an office in Seattle. This girl intrigued me — hiking alone, carrying a gun, and looking as if a puff of smoke would whisk her away!

"Why are you armed?" I asked.

"Well, before my husband went out he taught me to shoot so I can protect the children and myself. He said I must never go anywhere without a gun on account of the bears."

This astounded me. No one had ever mentioned bears. Harry had assured me there were no bears in the district. As Bernice strode off I told her that if she was ever in need of help we would go over. I often thought of this courageous woman alone in the bush. How I would have loathed it without Harry.

We had learned a lot from the previous winter, and were busy storing up supplies of vegetables, flour, sugar, tea, bottled fruits and berries. So one day in late summer when we were going over to the hay quarter I was delighted to see some particularly good high bush cranberries.

"I'll stop here and gather some," I told Harry.

"You can pick me up on this spot on your way back."

The berries were red and juicy, and I was constantly lured on by fruit-laden bushes further and further away. I continued to fill my basket when it suddenly dawned on me that I had been roaming haphazardly. I was panic-stricken. I tried to remember all the things I had been told about what to do when lost in the bush. I looked for the moss on the north side of the trees; but all I could think about was bears and the fact that I was lost. There was no sign of the trail at all.

The picking was forgotten and I was very scared. It seemed hours before I heard the sound of wagon wheels. Then I found I was quite close to the trail and had evidently been going round in circles as I was in nearly the same place where Harry had left me. But the fear of bears still lingered in my mind.

Mrs. Keltie, my long-time neighbour and by now a firm friend, showed me where to pick blueberries in the jack pine patch. With a runny-nosed child under one arm and a twenty-pound lard pail tied around her middle, she could outpick anyone in the district with one hand. Had a medal been awarded for berry picking Mrs. K. would have won the gold. I was most impressed but knew I couldn't compete with her.

Mrs. K. was also the uncrowned kraut queen of the district. A large, stinking barrel stood outside her front door to testify to this. She grew enough cabbages to have put *Mrs. Wiggs of the Cabbage Patch* out of the running — enough in fact to feed an entire army!

Mrs. K., who was most generous, arrived at our door one day with a large knife in one hand, and cabbages galore, salt and a barrel in her buggy. "I've come to make you kraut," she announced.

There was no use telling her I hated the stuff and didn't want to encourage any more mosquitoes or livestock around our door. She produced a huge supply and must have thought we had devoured it with relish as it was soon buried deep in the earth! Possibly we got rid of it too quickly as I heard of one person suffering from severe eczema who had accidentally plunged his arm into a barrelful of kraut and was mercifully cured — or perhaps it was the salt pork. Who was I to discount anything I heard?

Mrs. K's husband was a councillor and the only man left in the district who could sign his name after the young settlers had gone to the war. He was something like a character from Gilbert and Sullivan's *HMS Pinafore,* and filled all the positions of authority. He later became reeve which sounded important but caused him much trouble. Had royalty paid us a visit he would have risen to the occasion and found a red carpet, even if Mrs. K. had to knit it for him!

Mr. Keltie wallowed in protocol and it was amusing to see him swell up with his knowledge. He would have been capable of filling a city position had one been offered him.

Discussing his oratory I told him, "It's all in the way you hold your mouth." He immediately became worried that there was something wrong with his. Out came his wad of tobacco; he worked his jaws sideways, then up and down. Looking in the mirror he said, "Can't see nothin' wrong with me mouth."

At this time an election for reeve was announced, and Wilbur Keltie was up for re-election. I was appointed poll clerk, receiving my instructions from the incumbent. Voting was held in our school house. Sitting in a draughty schoolroom with a scrutineer breathing heavily down my neck, fully aware of his responsibility, was a very trying experience.

After our detailed briefing, Wilbur, smiling broadly, shouted in a voice that shook the none-too-safe rafters, "When I'm elected we'll have a dance tonight in this 'ere school house."

At the close of the poll the count was disastrous for him, the result being twenty-three for Keltie, twenty-four for Knowe. Recount after recount ensued, with Mr. Keltie carefully checking, but he couldn't change the result. In a raging temper he again raised the roof, shouting, "There'll be no dance in this 'ere school house tonight." After pausing for the catcalls he added, "Remember, I'm still chairman of this school board."

The victor had to bow to Mr. Keltie's ultimatum, but he organized a dance in a nearby barn where they had a good old booze-up. It was such heaven to go home to bed. To hell with their dance; I'd had enough.

Mr. Keltie's family looked after the farm and did all the work while he supervised the road work. A homesteader was allowed to work with his team grading roads, etc., and in lieu of wages he could take a percentage off his taxes; anything to save the cash they didn't have.

One amusing incident occurred when the school teacher insisted that the pupils call him "Sir". If a pupil was unable to attend school the usual note from a parent was necessary. Mrs. K. gave her son a note one day as follows:

Sir Lumstall
Kenneth helped with spring seeding that's why he don't show up at school. O.K. eh?
Lady Wilbur Keltie

155

"If he can be called 'Sir' then I can be called 'Lady'," said Mrs. K.

We were so busy with our own affairs that I had had no time to call on any of the new settlers, although my intentions were good. One day a young lad about ten years old came through our yard on his pony. He was on his way for mail and told us his father had gone out to make a grub stake. He added that his mother was very worried as she was having trouble with bears and was scared they would attack the children. It was very unnerving to think of these women being scared of bears, particularly when there were none in the district.

To allay my anxiety Harry said, "They must be imagining this bear scare."

A few hours later this same boy galloped into our yard, pleading with us to go to their help. "A bear has dragged one of our calves over the corral," he said. "The cattle are all upset and mum is frantic."

Of course we downed tools and went into immediate action. We saddled our horses and Harry took his gun. I also grabbed a .22, feeling most apprehensive about the whole affair and not at all sure what I could do with it. Buster followed us as usual.

On arrival at the homestead there was great excitement. The cattle in the corral were all bawling, and the boy's mother, Mrs. Witovski, told us of how for several nights she had seen the footprints of bears outside the house, and had actually heard them.

There was no doubt that a bear had dragged the calf right over a high corral. We sized up the situation — I from a long-range viewpoint. Harry followed a trail of blood and found a calf not far from the house with its shoulder half eaten away. He took up a position on top of the barn, figuring the bear would come back either for another calf or for the remainder of its spoil. Time went on and it began to get dark. It seemed senseless to wait any longer as he couldn't shoot without getting a proper aim.

Mrs. Witovski pleaded with us not to leave them and to spend the night. I was appalled at the thought but she was so upset. "Do stay. You can have my bed," she said.

Naturally I weakened and knew we couldn't desert them at a time like this. The bed was in a small cupboard-like room. Just above the head of the bed was a window. It had no glass but was covered with a piece of cheesecloth to keep out the mosquitoes.

Buster followed us into the bedroom and settled under the bed. In spite of wishing myself anywhere in the world than in this poky place, I was so exhausted mentally and physically that I fell asleep as soon as my head touched the pillow.

In the middle of the night I sensed something unusual. Buster was making a peculiar noise under the bed.

Shaking Harry I whispered, "Get up. The bear's here!"

He was used to my nightmares and was very tired. So he turned over and murmured, "Oh be quiet. You're dreaming. Go back to sleep; you've got bears on the brain."

"No Harry, listen to Buster. He knows the bear is here."

Still unconvinced, Harry refused to budge. He eventually persuaded me that I had been dreaming, and so we settled down once more.

The next morning Harry inspected the land around the house and found fresh bear tracks in the sandy soil under our bedroom window, with claw marks torn in the cheesecloth just above the head of our bed. He figured that the bear, standing

157

on its hind legs, would be at least six feet tall. While we'd been arguing that there was no bear it had been standing there with its claws a few feet from our faces, no doubt listening to our conversation.

We had to go home next morning to attend to our own stock. The only thing we could do was to alert as many as we could to be on the lookout.

That same night at dusk Tom Evatt, a bachelor who lived a mile or so away from our house, heard a rustling outside his shack door. He had been pulling carrots and had left a pile on the porch. On opening the door he was confronted by a huge black bear silhouetted against the light, busily eating his carrots.

He quietly picked up his gun in one hand and an oil lamp in the other and aimed, slamming the door quickly as he didn't know whether the shot had been fatal. He saw the bear run off and knew he couldn't go after it in the semi-darkness. Early the next morning he found it lying dead in a ditch nearby.

Tom called for help to skin and butcher it, and the men from the neighbouring homesteads decided they wanted a bear meat dinner. One of them brought a huge roast for me to cook which I shot into the oven protesting that no way would I eat any of it. In fact no one could stomach it as it had not been properly butchered and stank to high heaven. Apparently the bear had been ready to hibernate and its fat was about five inches thick.

I was instructed to render the fat which I was told was "as sweet as a nut". Then the fun started. What was I to do with all this fat? We gave lard pails of it away. Everyone who came had a new use for bear grease. We rubbed it in our hair, on our boots, on our saddles, and some of them on their chests. We also fried doughnuts and potatoes in it,

and made pastry and soap. The uses seemed endless.

We heard no more of bears in the district so we
felt sure this one had been the trouble-maker. Its
hide was tanned and hung from the gable of Tom's
shack. We could have had it for ten dollars, but not
possessing that much money it was impossible.

Apart from causing a lot of excitement, this bear
episode had taken precious time out of our arduous
work schedule as we still had to do so much before
freeze-up.

31
Proposing Charlie

We gloated over our crop. It was a firm, heavy
stand and ripened with the moon. Harvest time arrived; the wheat was ready to cut. Harry went forth
with his scythe, and when he had completed the
reaping a neighbour came in to help us, bringing
his binder. The homesteaders were kind hearted
and generous, lending each other equipment, and
giving a helping hand whenever possible. How
proud we were of the lovely golden stooks.

Then the threshing crew arrived, a small one
compared to the big outfit I had cooked for on the
ranch. But with our small cook stove and such limited space it was enough for me to cope with.

Our crop yielded about twenty-five bushels to
the acre. As we had only five acres it was little
enough. We took some of our wheat to a small grist
mill and brought home flour and cereal grains; no

need for added vitamins. The rest we used for cattle fodder. How simply and gratefully we lived — or should I say existed.

Life on the homestead was really toughening me. I started out by speaking gently to the cattle; now I found the way to get the herd moving was at the end of a pitchfork. The first time I saw this method it made me shudder, but I soon realized we had too much to do to stop and coax-on an ornery cow.

This second winter was another heller! Hay and feed were scarce throughout the district, especially as the Soldiers' Settlement loan had enabled and encouraged settlers to buy cattle and horses.

News went the rounds that "the Holmes have plenty of hay". Counting heads in the barn one cold night we found we had twenty-eight cows, horses, colts and calves to be fed and watered every day, including our five milk cows. We would never have qualified for a government-inspected milk shed. I realize now how primitive and unsanitary our operation was compared with today's high standards.

Hay was again hauled the six-mile round trip from the hay quarter. We took the two racks, and this year I was on the alert, and not nearly as nervous. Then again, I had my gun — just in case of trouble. This was a colossal undertaking, but it was exhilarating and exciting to hear the pistol-shot cracks as the trees split with the frost. The muskegs were heavy with snow, and smoke was rising from them. They were on fire and smouldered all the time — winter and summer.

Our fencing work had to stop as the ground froze solid to a depth of at least six feet. As the temperature plunged we had to move our bed downstairs because the second storey was too cold. Our second winter was as severe as our first one! The old-timers were right when they used the rammed earth design for their shacks, and the Eskimos knew what they were doing when they built their igloos.

The cold weather played havoc with my bread making. I received many helpful hints from my neighbours who impressed on me the importance of keeping it warm. To see the blasted dough rising in our easy chair by the stove, covered with my fur coat, was positively nauseating. It looked like a bloated old man.

Harry insisted that I go out with him when possible and not remain in the house alone. This was fine by me but interrupted my household chores. One day when I was in the midst of bread making he asked me to drop everything and help him in the barn.

"What about the bread?" I asked.

"Push it down and get your coat on," Harry replied.

"I can't. I've already pushed it down twice."

"Well, do it for the third time of asking."

I dutifully obeyed him, but when we opened the door on our return the dough hit us in the face! It was a particularly light batch and would no doubt sell at quite a high price today as sourdough bread.

During this time Harry had been coaxed into accepting the position of secretary to the local school board. They held long, tedious meetings, spending hours arguing over the location of a well or the appointment of a new teacher. Harry finally decided on a way to cut them short, so he filled the oil lamp with just enough oil to last as long as he thought the business on hand warranted. That was a most successful move!

The school was closed in the severest weather, and a list of pupils and reports had to be submitted.

There were of course no phones, and it was impossible to call at all the homes. In one report the names of the children of a new Russian immigrant had to be filled in. We knew there were four girls, and as the temperature was forty below zero Harry thought we could christen them by our own stove. So he filled in Cora, Dora, Flora, Nora.

This white lie went completely out of his mind until, at a school board meeting in the spring, his report was produced and the names Cora, Dora, Flora and Nora were called out. At this, the irate father jumped up and yelled, "Youse can't do this to me Mr. Man. I've got four girls already — Nina, Anastasia, Tanya and little Olga."

The matter was eventually straightened out; in any case Harry had been spared a long, cold trip.

Brook, the ex-Guardsman living nearby, was losing his stock in this cold weather. Every time he called on us he would tell us of another death. Harry said, "How can you expect to keep them alive, feeding them frozen slough grass?"

It was no good talking to Brook; he hadn't a clue. Besides he had another problem on his mind. His sister, a well-known authoress who had a villa in Italy and an estate in Ireland, wanted to visit Canada, take a trip to the Rockies and stay with her brother on his ranch in Alberta.

I had seen his shack, a low one-roomed dump with a sod roof. What he had led her to believe, or what she had built up in her mind, I don't know. She could never have envisioned such a crude home for her dear brother.

Plucking up his courage, he asked, "Mrs. Holmes, could you possibly put my sister up when she comes?"

How about that? Entertain a V.I.P.? Heaven forbid!

"Why don't you try to get her to pay your way out and meet her in the Rockies?" I replied.

It was a good idea but she didn't fall for it and decided not to visit Canada after all. So that was one more problem solved.

We were having troubles with our own cattle, and Harry was doing his best to cope. The first cow he had to shoot was like killing a relative — awful! But later on, as more animals were landed on us, usually limping in and half-starved, Harry would come in, take the gun off the wall and look at me. I'd nod my head. Another shot; one less mouth to feed.

The chickens were doing well as we had managed to get their house fixed. They survived the winter in great shape. They were Rhode Island Reds, providing a bright touch of colour against the white snow, and delivering delicious large eggs.

A new young school teacher arrived from Edmonton that winter to take over the nearby one-room school. She boarded with a farmer on the quarter adjoining our homestead, and visited me often. She was very depressed, being nervous and highly strung, and was quite unable to cope with the wild kids of the district and the extreme cold. Some of her pupils were taller than she, and not much younger. Poor Minnie didn't last very long and went out suffering from a nervous breakdown. It was so senseless of the education department to send young, inexperienced girls such as her into this untamed wilderness.

Stories of moonshine parties were abundant. Most of the settlers brewed their own liquor. One man, known as the Moonshine King, matured his brew in his manure pile, as did the old rascal Tump Evans. The Moonshiner came to a sad end, and one very like Tump's own. While drunk in his shack one bitterly cold night he somehow contrived to set fire to the place and he was burned to a cinder!

On another occasion a wild card party was in progress. All the players were drunk and each had a gun. One fellow lost his temper and he and his host had a shoot-out that scattered the guests, who quickly left for home. A little way along the trail another of the merrymakers said, "Hell, I've left my hat!" He went back for it, opened the shack door, grabbed his headgear and put it on his head. Whereupon his erstwhile host raised his gun and shot him through the hat which mercifully saved his life.

There were so many strange happenings and conversations. I wish I could remember them all. One day a young fellow dropped in to see me. I knew his father had been sick so I asked, "How's your father, Salvo?"

"Oh, me dad's okay. He's out exposing hisself," he replied cheerfully. Evidently the first of the streakers! I never dared ask what people meant when they used unusual words.

There were so many bereavements in the district. Two widowers were left with seven children each. That made fourteen more motherless children to be cared for. Most of the deaths were caused by neglect at childbirth, and still the government will not allow midwives to be licensed in Canada. Why not, I wonder?

One young French Canadian mother of a large family told me stoically, "I will have one more only and then I will hand in my 'receipt'." Her 'receipt' was death on giving birth to her last child.

I almost began to lose my sense of humour which was vital to help me through these hard times. All for what? To prove up?

The three hundred and twenty acres of land (two quarters) seemed so marvellous to the average

Englishman. Most of the British Isles at that time was owned by the landed gentry. God knows we were no landed gentry, and we were still striving to get the three hundred and twenty acres. Little did we know that when we did have it, it was not "for the birds", but "for the rabbits"!

One day when Harry had to go out without me a little Frenchman called at the door.

"Where is your 'usband?" he enquired.

I told him Harry was clearing the bush. He didn't explain the reason for his visit but talked a lot about what a hard life it was and what disasters befell the settlers. I felt he had come with the grim intention of terrifying me, and he was making a good job of it.

He came closer and stared penetratingly into my eyes, saying, "This life is very dangerous for your 'usband. He could get killed, yes?"

Springing back in alarm, I cried, "Oh no!" Somehow I had never thought of anything happening to Harry. If it did, whatever would I do?

"Don't worry madame. I come and marry you, yes?"

Charlie was smiling and obviously very happy at this prospect. I felt like hitting out with the nearest weapon, which happened to be an axe, but managed to restrain myself. That would have been the last straw for my poor husband!

After his departure I nearly went to pieces. How dare a stranger frighten me like this! I knew too well the dangers of life in the bush. How thankful I was to see my beloved husband walk in safe and sound.

When I told him about the caller he laughed and said, "Oh yes, that's Proposing Charlie. He goes around the district proposing to all the women. He's an old bachelor and really quite harmless."

165

32
Shacking Up with Daisy

Christmas came and went — another New Year to face, just as cold and unrelenting. Magazines, papers and letters from home were the highlights of our long winter evenings. Harry had built book-shelves across one end of our room to hold our pre-cious books and pieces of pottery. The fact that you got a sliver every time you reached for some read-ing matter was incidental. Everything was home-spun — true Canadiana!

In early February Brook rode in on his little pony. He was frantic! Bursting through our door and trip-ping over the threshhold, he shouted breathlessly, "I've bad news! Daisy's dying!"

"Oh no, not Daisy," I cried. "She's all you've got left."

Brook begged us to go over to his place immedi-ately, so although we were up to our eyes with chores we promised to follow as soon as we had hitched up our team to a hayrack on the sleigh. As he cantered off, Harry calmly rolled a cigarette and considered the matter carefully as he always did. He said he would throw a few sheaves of oats and some hay into the wagon, which we could ill spare. He figured it might be some hours before we got home, and he was indeed right. Buster scampered after us, wondering what we were in for now. He had a very high IQ and did everything but talk.

When we arrived, Daisy was lying flat on the fro-zen ground rolling her eyes piteously. Her new-born calf was frisking around, apparently in good health.

Daisy was the sole survivor of the herd which

Brook had purchased with his Soldiers' Settlement loan — the last of the Mohicans! We realized that she must be saved at all cost as the inspector had sent him further warnings about his heavy cattle losses and was beginning to ask very awkward questions.

Harry, in his old army tunic and Sam Browne belt, took charge of the situation and issued the orders.

First he took a look in the small, roofless log barn in which the manure was piled high, as Brook had had the bright idea of turning the cattle round from time to time to save cleaning it out.

"If we are to save Daisy she will have to be kept warm," said Harry. We all looked at each other; Brook's shack with its sod roof was the only answer.

Brook gazed helplessly at Daisy then gallantly agreed. "Okay, it's all I can do for her."

The shack was about eight by ten feet, with a bed, stove, table and a roughly constructed cupboard behind the door. We measured Daisy and found that by throwing out the cupboard we could fit part of her into the corner.

Harry stomped around in the snow and organized a plan of action. "Brook, you move the cabinet, washbasin and junk out of the corner."

Taking me aside he said, "Now Peggy, listen to me and do just what I say. I will unhitch Skin and Grief and attach them to a logging chain through the small side window. Then I'll pull the chain, with a rope on the end, through the door and haul Daisy inside by her neck."

Brook had been listening uneasily. "Which way will her head be?" he enquired dubiously.

"Make your choice, and quickly," said Harry.

"Well I'd prefer her head next to my bed."

This was good thinking! Harry threw a bed of straw in the corner and prepared the intensive care ward. Operation No. 1 went into action.

"Put the rope around Daisy's neck," he commanded, "and I'll take the team to the other side of the cabin."

I had to give Harry the orders to "get up" or to "whoa". Brook was no use in an emergency.

Everything was in order. I shouted "get up" and Daisy began to slide along the frozen ground. Her head was just over the sill when Brook suddenly yelled "whoa" and streaked past me into the shack, coming out with a small enamel mug, whereupon he knelt on the ground and started feverishly to milk her.

Harry was waiting impatiently for my signal to restart, and came round from his side of the building to see what was holding up operations.

"What the devil's going on?" he thundered. I replied, "He's milking Daisy."

Harry's language, usually very controlled, completely deserted him. "In the name of the Almighty," he roared, "he's robbing the dead!"

Brook rose, stretched his long legs, and showing me half a mug of milk said with delight, "Thank God she's not dry, Mrs. Holmes."

This had delayed proceedings and we had to start all over again. This time Brook helped me guide the sliding cow into her new abode where she lay like a half-dead queen, not in a draughty barn but a cosy maternity home! She seemed to appreciate all we were doing for her, and let out a moo — just a weak one — but all the same a moo!

One would think that we could pat ourselves on the back and call it a day, but oh no! We had to look further ahead. How would Brook get her up on her feet each day? To leave her lying in her weakened state would be fatal. By this time he was willing to risk his life to save Daisy — anything at all not to have to face the angry inspector and report another death.

Harry tested the rafters and thought they might hold. In any case we had to take a chance. So he sent me back to our quarter for a pulley and winch, and some straps to put under her belly. Brook was to put the rope around the beam and out through the door, and attach it to the horn of the pony's saddle. He would then move the pony forward, which would hopefully raise Daisy off the ground.

We tested Operation No. 2 which seemed to work, so with the rope in position, a blanket under her belly, and strict instructions to Brook on how to perform the lift, we left the odd roommates.

Daisy was snugly settled in her corner, with her frisky offspring running around outside, and Brook was fully prepared to spend the rest of his days nursing Daisy back to health — with feed provided by the Holmes!

Exhausted and fed up we returned home hours later for our own chores, and our herd was bellowing for food and water.

About noon the next day Brook arrived with a satisfied smirk on his face. "Tell me, how did you get on with Daisy in the night?" I asked.

"Fine, Mrs. Holmes, once I got used to her hot breathing." Being a bachelor he wasn't used to breath on his face!

He added that he nearly fell out of bed when for no apparent reason she let out one of her moos. But he had managed, without pulling the roof on top of them, to haul her up onto her feet.

This shacking up with Daisy lasted harmoniously for weeks — in fact until the snow began to disappear in April. By this time Daisy was strong enough to walk outside alone and nibble on the new tender green leaves. But she was thoroughly spoiled and housetrained, and insisted on returning home to the cow palace — her moo-tel — each night.

As the days got longer and warmer, water was in the sloughs and the grass began to grow, so Brook foolishly let her stay out altogether, until one day he found her down again. We had to haul her back into the cabin and the whole proceedings started over again.

Then she had a relapse. Brook should have put her out of her misery but she was the only asset he had left to show the Soldiers' Settlement Board. But by this time she was too frail to be pulled up and down.

In May Brook had to go to town on business and asked us to pop over to feed her. Armed with fodder we drove over and found her in a bad state; she had developed bed sores, poor pet. We dressed the sores with antiseptic but knew the end was near. Next day she was dead.

That same day he called in on us on his way home from town and we gave him the sad news. As he stretched out by our well-stoked stove he leaned back saying, "Well I did my best for her. I've no regrets, but what the hell shall I do now?"

He had no possible way of repaying his loan and we decided it would be better for him to give up farming, as he had gone out of it whether he liked it or not. "Pull out," Harry advised him. "Leave the province and don't let anyone know where you are."

So Brook went home to bury Daisy and collect his belongings. He brought us his pony and calf to look after, and once again our family was increased.

Before leaving, he asked me to do him one more favour. Would I please cut his hair? As I was the official barber of the district and by now quite handy

170

with the scissors, I obliged. I always seemed to get a better effect on the front, but I obviously pleased my customers.

Thus another defeated homesteader joined the club. It was several months before we had a letter from him telling us he was in a mental institution in Manitoba.

"Heavens," I exclaimed, "they've caught up with him at last!"

But my fears were unfounded. He informed us later that he was an attendant at the hospital, and was just off "to take the King of Spain to hoe spuds."

Brook stayed there until his retirement, remaining a bachelor all his life. Daisy was his only bedfellow!

33
Shattered Dreams

Winter! How I came to hate the word, but spring lifted our hearts, and when the creeks began to sing we once again thawed out and were full of life and hope.

By now we were the cattle kings of the district. All the S.S.B. inspector would have to do would be to visit our place and book us on charges of cattle stealing. We could have counterclaimed for room and board for the unwanted herd; but no one came. I guess the Soldiers' Settlement Board had also given up the struggle.

Our winter hay hauling stint was over, but we

had lots of spring work to begin. Fencing was still No. 1 on the list as the government demanded that a specified amount of fencing be done, along with other improvements to the land, before the title was clear.

Our intention was merely to prove up the land on which Harry had filed, to stay two years and then return to England. I don't think I could have stuck it if it hadn't been for that wonderful end-of-the-rainbow dream. It was strange that we built such a large, solid house as if we were destined to spend our lives in it.

Letters from home at this time were very disturbing. We were told that my father had not been well but was recovering. However, business reverses had hit the family. My eighty-year-old grandfather was also sick, and living conditions were changing for the comfortable British middle-class. The postwar depression was reaching a peak, taxes were unbelievably high, and people were talking of emigrating.

We could see our promise to return home in two years fading into thin air. My folks didn't actually advise us not to come, but they hinted that they might like to go to Canada themselves.

My enthusiasm for this tough life was waning, and I began to wonder what was in store for us. By April I knew I was pregnant again. This would mean a trip to the city when the child was due as I wouldn't dare take a chance by remaining in the bush without medical help, especially after the tragic loss of our first baby.

The prospect of my parents joining us in Canada didn't give us the joy it should have done. We had no idea what we could do if we had to leave the homestead, and there would be no room for both of them here.

Meanwhile plans were going ahead in England.

My father's doctor thought a sea trip would be the very best thing for his health after his "slight stroke". This was the first time the word "stroke" had been mentioned, which alarmed me. The letter also contained a definite sailing date in May. Dad was to travel alone and my mother would follow, after disposing of the business and attending to other family commitments.

It was too late to let them know of our plight; we had to face up to this sudden change in our lives. We had accepted everything blow by blow, but I just couldn't visualize my father in this rustic setting. A sudden introduction to our way of life might be disastrous for him. He was used to city life, his club, theatres and sports. He was no outdoors man and had never had an inclination to farm or to live in the country.

Our new problems seemed insurmountable and we had to make and remake our plans to cope with the situation. We were near to completing our necessary improvements in order to get clear title to the land, so we decided that dad should spend the summer with us on the homestead and accompany us to the city when we left for the birth of our baby.

How true is the saying, "Man proposes, God disposes." It is a blessing that fate does not reveal the future. We would never be able to take it!

As the sailing date had already been set, we had little time to complete all our arrangments. One of the most important was toilet facilities. I had a small chemical "Ladies" in the house, but there was nothing for the men. I decided this would be my project as Harry had to get on with the fencing.

First of all, in order to make a separate bedroom for dad, we built a partition to divide our large bedroom which occupied the whole of the second

173

storey. Then I sized up the building site for the toilet.

I was delighted to find two trees growing strategically near the barn. By closing in two sides between the trees, using the barn as the third wall, I thought it should be easy to construct an effective triangular affair. By working union hours plus overtime, and using an inordinate number of six-inch spikes, I completed my building operation and stood back proudly to survey my handiwork. Chick Sales, the humourist of that time who wrote an amusing book on toilets, certainly never had a three-cornered one like mine. In my opinion it was a masterpiece!

We purchased a chemical toilet from the local store, which we placed in position as carefully as a royal throne. A horse blanket draped over a pole made an improvised entrance. It was very primitive, but private, and at least original!

There wasn't much else to be done to show our affection for father. The sailing date in the letter had been the knock of doom. Father was to sail from Liverpool to Montreal, and travel via the Canadian Pacific Railway to Edmonton where he would have to be met. Harry couldn't leave, so a neighbour offered to take me in his wagon to St. Paul where the railroad started. Harry arranged for one of his army buddies, Jimmie Dunstall, who had given up homesteading, to meet me in Edmonton and to put me up while I was there.

My city clothes were brought out into the light of day. Fortunately I had a navy-blue tailored suit and could always make a hat out of any odd bit of material around the house. It seemed strange to dress up once again. I had worn riding pants and sweaters during the winter, and long, loose cotton dresses in the summer, and I felt uncomfortable in conventional attire. How wonderful it would have been had I lived in the jeans age.

Harry had a bad attack of lumbago just before I left. It was the first time he had been sick. It was bad enough to travel without him, but to see him in pain and not be able to help was most upsetting. Moreover, I had a strange presentiment about this journey which was long and tedious; the train stopped at every whistle stop. I felt very conspicuous as my outfit was one which I had brought from England in 1919. Little Orphan Annie had nothing on me! But I had a book to read, and was looking forward to a pleasant uninterrupted respite from work. A young man living near us had arranged for his mother to introduce herself to me when she boarded the train at Radway Centre, so we could have a friendly, womanly chat.

Waiting with me in line at the ticket office was a kind-looking, middle-aged man with a clerical collar who gallantly offered to carry my bag and help me aboard. I sat at the rear of the coach and the minister stationed himself at the front on the opposite side. We were the only people in the compartment.

At last the train bell clanged, and with much chugging we took off. Taking off my hat and jacket I settled myself in a window seat with my book. I was absorbed in the story and didn't notice the minister until he was in the seat by my side. He asked endless personal questions which I fended off, hoping he would go away and leave me in peace. Getting no encouragement he eventually toddled back to his seat, and with a sigh of relief I was soon deep in my book again.

Heck! Here he was again by my side, snuggling as close as he could. I showed him that he was not welcome but nothing deterred this old nut. His

175

conversation became more and more suggestive, with obvious double meanings. I began to wonder whether I was bushed and if I really understood him. Over and over again he begged me to confide in him.

"I know you are running away from your husband," he said. "Have you been ill-treated? Do you need help?"

"No, of course not!" I replied indignantly.

"Have you any children?"

"No."

Then he rolled his eyes towards heaven murmuring, "Well, perhaps I can help you with that problem."

"There's no problem. Please leave me alone. I want to read my book."

But he insisted. "I could take you to a home," he said.

I began to wonder if I were mixed up in some white slave traffic deal. What in the name of God was the matter with this man? He became more offensive and was obviously a sex maniac. I told him once more to leave me alone as he was annoying me, and looked up at the alarm signal wondering whether I should stop this noisy, slow-moving train. But he sensed my intention, smiled sardonically and, much to my relief, returned to his seat.

Just then the conductor of the train came along. I told him excitedly that I'd been insulted, and tried to explain what had taken place without being too explicit.

"Quieten down young lady," he laughed. "That's your story. You don't expect me to believe you!" Then he approached the so-called minister, said something to him, and they began to roar with laughter. Apparently it was a big joke and they were buddies!

We made one long stop at Radway where more

freight and passengers were taken on. To my relief, a group of farm lads entered the coach. Safe now, I could collect my wits. One of the boys across the aisle played a mouth organ; another had a fiddle. He scraped and the others sang in harmony. My spirits began to rise again.

Mrs. Feber, the lady I was expecting to meet, also boarded the train at Radway, introduced herself and sat next to me. Being full of my unnerving experience I spilled out the whole story to her. The minister was still in the coach.

But Mrs. Feber looked at me sternly and said, "I think you've been in the bush too long. You don't expect me to believe that story. Look at his collar; he's a minister."

By this time I began to doubt my sanity and picked up my book again, having nothing in common with my companion. Then the minister strolled down the aisle and stopped before the musicians. He took the fiddle from one youth and began to play — incidentally very well. Then, like a Hungarian violinist serenading a loved one in some romantic rendezvous, he leaned across Mrs. Feber, ignoring her and gazed into my eyes. "This I play for you alone, my darling."

In a rage I turned to Mrs. Feber. "Now do you believe me?"

"Yes I do," she replied. "But let me tell you he's not really a minister. I think I've heard about him before."

Jimmie Dunstall duly met me in Edmonton and I could scarcely get out my greeting before I said, "You see that minister? Well, I'm going to report him to the police."

"Calm yourself, Peggy," said Jimmie. "You've been in the bush too long. You can't start doing that sort of thing as soon as you come to the city."

Although I had been living in the wilds with

many desperate characters all around me, I realized how protected I had been, and so I calmed down. But I was out to defend all young girls. When I look at them today I can see that they are not the dupes we were.

My father was not expected for two days so it was grand having a chance to visit our friends the Andisons, the popular "Uncle Bob", Clerk of the Legislative Assembly in the Alberta Government, and his charming Scots wife, Emily. To be able to talk about things other than homestead chores was a real joy. It was too bad Harry couldn't have taken the trip with me to get a break.

Edmonton was just a small town with poor roads and street cars on the tracks, but it seemed a huge, bustling metropolis to me. Train arrivals were somewhat haphazard; Monday's train might come after Tuesday's, for instance. Everything was taken very casually.

We had no definite notification of the time of arrival of passengers from Dad's boat, but on the scheduled day I went down to the station early. No sign of him. I returned to the Dunstalls where I was staying, thinking he would be on the next train. I met every train for nine days, but there was no sign of him. On the fourth day some passengers from the boat alighted in Edmonton. I spoke to as many as I could, but they said that although they remembered Mr. Lewis no one had any news about him. One man told me he had definitely left the train in eastern Canada. I was desperately worried; I had no means of consulting with Harry as there were no phones or radios to keep us in touch. Each day was the same story. The CPR officials were sympathetic, but after clearing customs in Montreal the passengers were on their own.

My friends took turns in escorting me to the station, and at last, on the tenth day, I saw my father in the distance. He was a shadow of the man I'd left a few years before. He was like a child when he put his arms around me and told me his story. All I could think of was, thank God he is safe.

He apparently remembered all about the sea voyage which he had enjoyed, also clearing customs in Montreal and getting onto the train. About a day later he had a blackout, and when he recovered consciousness he was in a hospital in some small place in eastern Canada; he had no idea where. His first thought was that he was in a mental institution as he had never seen screen wire on a window before. He kept very quiet and watched the others in the ward. Everyone seemed normal and the nurses didn't treat him as if he were insane; and he was relieved to find he wasn't in a straitjacket. The nursing staff had been very kind to him and took the money for his expenses from his wallet, explaining the currency. Then they put him on the train for Edmonton.

I was so happy to be reunited at last, and my main preoccupation was to get him to the homestead as soon as possible, that I didn't think things out as clearly as I should. That's where Harry would have taken over. I asked him if he would like to see a doctor but he wouldn't hear of it. I should have insisted, of course, and I should also have taken time for a medical examination for myself; but I was feeling very well and we mothers-to-be in the north didn't bother about pre-natal clinics — in any case there weren't any. This neglect might have saved us another heartbreak when I lost twin daughters in early January of the following year.

Dad was interested in the countryside and the journey back to St. Paul was definitely less eventful than my journey out. I had managed to get word to Harry with a homesteader going into the area that we were on the way, and I hoped he would be at St. Paul when we arrived. However, he didn't receive the news in time to meet the train so we had another delay before taking off. It was wonderful to see him again and to hear that his lumbago had cleared up.

Dad was astounded when he saw the horse team which was to take him on the last lap of his journey. It was quite a task hauling him onto the high seat, and he was amazed to think he would have to ride over thirty miles on that hard board.

Just as we were ready to pull away, a meek and mild little man asked if we could give him a lift as he was going to our part of the country.

"Okay, climb in," said Harry. He never could refuse to do a favour. Our unknown passenger had a faraway look in his eyes and we couldn't get any information out of him at all. He came with us nearly the whole way, and stopped off at the post office house at Sugden. We thought no more of him.

Dad was numb by the time we reached our journey's end.

"Well, here's The Gables. How do you like it?" I asked with pride. His mouth opened in amazement. He had never conjured up anything like this from my description of our home.

He took one long look, then turning to me with pity said, "Oh my dear, how can you stand it?"

We felt shaken and beaten, and wondered how on earth he would fit into the picture. We were dog tired, and the next morning I was very sick. All the emotion and strain had hit me with a delayed action. It would have been easy to die at that point!

Dad's next surprise was his special toilet. I directed him to my building masterpiece. He returned saying, "What in heaven's name is that place — no roof, a gale blowing and a damned

180

horse blanket flapping around my knees." He didn't appreciate it at all.

The man to whom we had given a lift turned out to be an evangelist — a hell and damnation firebrand. He went around telling the farmers that the end of the world was near and they needn't worry about work; it would all be in vain. Some of the men believed him and neglected their crops and stock.

One evening the evangelist held a meeting in our school house, and as we had heard a lot about his haranguing, and having been responsible for bringing him into the district, we decided to attend.

He raved for nearly an hour, and then went round to speak to each person in the room. Dad sat next to me and I heard the man ask him, "Are you saved?" I was taken aback when dad replied, *"We* know, don't we?"

34
And So Farewell

Summertime, and living should be easy — but not for us! Our problems had been multiplied with the arrival of father. We would have needed a computer to analyse our financial situation, but of course we had never heard of computers then!

Our next project was pigs! We thought it would be good to go in for pigs as it would make a welcome change of menu and we hoped to get a good price for them. We had already started to build a pig pen. The slabs were lying on the ground and the posts were in.

So one day when Harry was in the bush, I decided to surprise him and finish the job myself. The result was solid and imposing, although Harry scolded me for using too many six-inch spikes. However, the slabs never came off, not like those placed on Edmonton City Hall many years later. The court case which resulted was headlined in the press as "The Slobs That Put On The Slabs."

So we purchased six of the cutest little piglets from a farmer some miles away which Harry brought home triumphantly in our wagon. However, during the unloading they somehow managed to escape and scampered off into the bush.

It didn't look as if it would be much trouble to round them up, but although Harry and a couple of hefty neighbours chased them round and round for an hour or so, they were defeated, and returned to the house to cool off while the pigs remained at liberty, fresh as young whippets.

I had been instructed to lock Buster up as the men thought he would only add to the confusion. The poor dog was most upset, barking and whining as he knew something unusual was going on.

Over a cup of tea the men planned a new campaign. They would set gopher traps and spread grain over them. This they did, covering a wide area. But the pigs were smarties; the only one to get caught was Tom Evatt who trod on a trap.

After another hour of fruitless effort they gave up the struggle. "Let Buster get at them," said Harry. "We've probably seen the last of them anyway." He was fed up to the teeth by this time.

So Buster was released and sprang out with glee. In about five minutes he had herded all the pigs into the pen. We had forgotten that he was an old ranch hand and very, very clever. Once inside the pen I knew they were safe because of my stalwart building effort. They were as good as bacon once that gate was shut.

As usual the animals became my pets, and the youngest piglet, just a wee one, I christened Desoline, after a homesteader who had left the district. I thought this was a nice name, never dreaming I would ever meet this lady again. But one can never take things for granted.

Forty years later this former neighbour unexpectedly looked us up in Edmonton. We dragged out the snap albums and had a great time talking about the bad old days. Mrs. Leclaire stopped when we came to the picture of my pet pig, which bore the caption Desoline. She gasped and said, "What a coincidence! That's my name."

Father continued to be a great anxiety as his health was obviously deteriorating. He wanted so much to help, but by the time he had changed into the appropriate clothes and polished his boots, Harry had taken off, done the job and was back home.

One day I gave dad a foaming pail of milk and said, "Will you please take this to the barn and give it to the calf."

About half an hour later he returned with the full pail.

"Why didn't you give it to the calf?" I asked.

"I couldn't, the calf was asleep."

So much for his help. We would take him into the bush with us as we didn't like to leave him alone all day. I of course had been carefully trained by Harry to stand where it was safe when he was felling a tree. But dad would grab me and pull me away, saying, "Come here, my dear. How does he know where the tree will fall?"

We had several close shaves, and realized that dad just wasn't cut out for our type of life.

He couldn't imagine why we worked non-stop and had no time to relax, except late at night when we dipped into our books.

"Why don't you play cards?" he enquired. I had always enjoyed a game of cards with him at home. He had taught me whist and considered me a promising player. "Many a man is selling matches on the streets of London today because he didn't play his trumps," he would inform me. But the idea of setting up a card table and wasting precious time from our chores just didn't occur to me.

However I did try to arrange some outdoor recreation, and fixed up a croquet lawn, if one could call it that. Although we cropped the grass as close as we could, the many bumps and dips forced us to use a golf club instead of a croquet mallet in order to whack the balls through my improvised hoops. This, as you may imagine, was not my father's idea of croquet.

We also tried to take him riding, as Mabel was a quiet steed, but by the time we had helped him to dress in suitable garb, adjusted the stirrups and hoisted him up, the effort wasn't worth while, as he tired all too soon.

One day we decided to take a little time off, so we arranged to go on a picnic with our friends the Kilfords. As we reached Beaver River Crossing, Harry and Arthur told us about the time, before World War I, when they were hired by the government to bring a hundred tamarack logs out of the bush for the construction of the first bridge over the river. They hauled the first loads of logs on sleighs, but the snow began to melt before they could get out the last load, so they used a wagon running gear. On the way down the hill to the river, where there was a sharp bend, the wagon hit a rock, turning the load over and pinning Arthur under it. He was badly bruised but happily not seriously injured.

Fortunately the bridge we had to cross for our picnic was a steel erection, as the old log one had been carried away by the ice some years before. So, singing and laughing, we made our way to Fork Lake about seven miles away. With a slow team it seemed a very long trip, but it was worth it, and Harry and I decided we must take a bit more time off in future. We were both young and we had so little fun.

When we arrived at the lake it was shimmering in the sunlight — a beautiful sight. It was about five miles long and shaped like a fork, hence its name. Now the lake is popular as a fishing and summer resort, but in those days it was unknown and deserted, except for the wildlife.

We spread a tablecloth on the ground and erected our mosquito bars — cheesecloth draped over posts — and managed to enjoy our feast despite all the pests.

That summer was sweltering, and the mosquitoes and black flies were worse than usual. The horses were covered with blood from the hundreds of bites, and I had to slap them with rags to keep them from stampeding. The poor cattle, too, were miserable, and would stand nodding their heads monotonously around the smudge — a fire which we fenced in and dampened down with wet leaves and hay so that it was constantly smoking. We put nose guards on them to help a little, but they suffered terribly.

I also began to wilt, and dad had several bad turns. Our fences were neglected and the cattle got into our crop. We could see the handwriting on the wall. We were beaten, although we refused to admit it!

After dad had had three more quite serious attacks we called Dr. Schoff, the old "Doc" at Beaver River Crossing, and asked him to ride out and see father. On examining him he said gravely, "Your father is very ill. He has high blood pressure, and you must get him to the city as soon as possible."

That was the first time we had heard of high blood pressure, and in those days we had no pills or medication to help such afflictions. Fortunately Harry and I had both kept very healthy, with never a cold, aided by our natural diet of herbs and vegetables. We had begun to forget many of the delicacies we had enjoyed in the past. Meat was scarce and we existed chiefly on rabbits. What I couldn't do with a rabbit once it had its fur off was nobody's business. I made stew, roast, ragout, fricassé, supplemented, of course, by plenty of fresh milk and eggs.

But we had to act on the doctor's advice. If only Harry could finish the fencing we could call it a day and leave the homestead. Harry was on the last pull of the line fence, another half mile to go on our south boundary. We had to get this finished or the land would not be ours. Harry refused to sell the property, even if he could, as he had hopes that oil would be found there. He was right, as it turned out, as oil drilling has recently begun in the area. Gas has already been found, and it is believed that there is plenty of oil there too. Of course, this was all too late for us, as by that time we were no longer the owners.

I went out to help Harry complete the fencing and, working feverishly against time, Harry made a pull with the wire stretchers when they slipped, and he had another bad gash to add to the scars from his previous mishaps.

We had just finished — and had proved up at last — when dad had another blackout. There was no time to waste.

"We must leave at once," said Harry. It was a great blow as we were at last beginning to make out, and I had adjusted myself to the rigours of a homestead life. However I agreed that we must be near a doctor, and Edmonton would be the place to go. Harry was a man who worked on hunches, and go we must. Father's health was now our chief concern, and we were both a little anxious about my pregnancy.

Leaving was like an amputation. A neighbour asked us if he could put in a crop and run his cattle on our land. We agreed, and cut ourselves off at once, no lingering farewells, no time to recoup financially. What furniture we could take we piled into the wagon, giving away many things to needy settlers. Another neighbour offered to sell our herd at the first opportunity.

Parting with the saddle horses, my little Mignon, Croquette and her family, Nip and Tuck our pet calves, was heartbreaking. And of course there was Mrs. Plymouth, the friendly hen. We couldn't possibly take her. Buster must, of course, go with us. He was almost human and remained part of our family for another fifteen years.

How quickly one digs oneself in, and how it hurts to uproot. We drove quickly away from our very own property which by now we had come to love, with Skin and Grief pulling our wagon for the last time, and Buster bounding behind us.

I turned to take a final look at our forlorn-looking home which had taken us so many months of hard labour to build, and the land which we had worked so desperately to clear. It reminded me of Tennyson's haunting lines:

> *Close the door, the shutters close,*
> *Or thro' the windows we shall see*
> *The nakedness and vacancy*
> *Of the dark deserted house.*

Come away; no more of mirth
Is here or merry-making sound.
The house was builded of the earth,
And shall fall again to ground.

"Oh Harry," I said. "Aren't you going to take a last look?"

"No," he replied firmly. "I never look back."

I'm afraid I did look back, like Lot's wife, but my eyes were blurred by tears. How hard we had slaved to make a new life, and now we would have to start all over again.

Jogging along the thirty-mile bumpy trail to Ashmont was a strain on my father, but he was in good humour and obviously pleased to be heading towards civilization. He could never understand how we could have "roughed" it for so long. He had missed his social life, his clubs, and card games with his friends.

On arrival at the rail terminal I patted Skin and Grief for the last time, shedding a few more tears. Buster looked up at us with pleading eyes. He knew our little world was changing. I flung my arms around him and told him, "Of *course* you're coming with us."

As he understood everything we said, he was overjoyed and bounded into the bush for the last time, returning to my heels as we boarded the slow mixed freight and passenger train, which stopped at every little station, loading and unloading squeaking pigs, people, and other cargo.

The journey to Edmonton took us twelve hours and gave me plenty of time to think about our future — although actually "to think" was the last thing I wanted to do. There were so many questions in my mind. But the homestead life had taught me not to jump my fences. Harry was very quiet throughout the journey, and I respected his silence.

Harry's old army buddy, Jimmie Dunstall, met us at the station and took us to his home until we could find a place of our own. I went absolutely wild at the sight of all the modern conveniences. I turned taps on and off, gazed enviously at the large oven, and then had one of the longest baths in my life. In fact, I lay in the water so long that Harry had to bang on the door to bring me back to reality.

Our first Edmonton home was a "castle" — a square building made of concrete blocks on the Ross Flats near the river. Most of the wooden houses in the area had been swept away in a recent flood, but luckily our house was solid enough to withstand the elements. To open my window and watch the river surging past was a new experience.

We still had to battle with an old stove, but we found coal on the river bank from the coal mines beneath. So instead of sawing logs, Harry dug out coal. We had running water and electricity and, although our home was humble and it would be quite a while before we could build ourselves a really nice house, we began to settle down.

The first radios appeared at this time, and we were the proud possessors of a little crystal set with one lead from the kitchen tap and the other attached to our bed spring. We were entranced at this novelty, although I groaned when the first music I heard was the *Anvil Chorus*. Evidently it was to be our theme song.

Father seemed better, and I sent an SOS for mother to join us from England. Our lives had indeed changed dramatically.

Although we had managed to prove up and obtain the title to our land, we had lost all our money — which hadn't been much to start with!

But we took a long time to uproot ourselves, and continued to pay taxes on the land for many years before giving up on it entirely. We eventually sold the home quarter for seven hundred dollars and the hay quarter for five hundred, minus the real estate man's commission.

Our sturdy home stood empty for fifty years, with no windows or doors, looking like a sightless old man. But the Englishman's dream of owning land had been fulfilled, and we had gained a lot of living experience which was to stand us in good stead in the years to come.